Using GPS

Finding Your Way with the Global Positioning System

Bruce Grubbs

FALCON®

HELENA, MONTANA

A FALCON GUIDE®

Falcon® is continually expanding its list of recreational guidebooks. All books include detailed descriptions, accurate maps, and all the information necessary for enjoyable trips. You can order extra copies of this book and get information and prices for other Falcon® guidebooks by writing Falcon, P.O. Box 1718, Helena, MT 59624 or calling toll-free 1-800-582-2665. Please ask for a free copy of our current catalog. Visit our website at www.FalconOutdoors.com or contact us by e-mail at falcon@falcon.com.

© 1999 Falcon® Publishing, Inc., Helena, Montana
Printed in Canada.

1 2 3 4 5 6 7 8 9 0 TP 04 03 02 01 00 99

Library of Congress Cataloging-in-Publication Data
Grubbs, Bruce (Bruce O.)
    Using GPS : finding your way with the Global Positioning
System / Bruce Grubbs.
        p.   cm.
    Includes bibliographical referneces and index.
    ISBN 1-56044-821-0 (pbk.)
    1. Global Positioning System. I. Title. II. Title: Using Global
Positions System.
G109.5.G78 1999
910' .285—dc21   98-50460
                                                                  CIP

CAUTION

Never use GPS, or any other system, as your sole means of navigation. Outdoor recreation activities are by their very nature potentially hazardous. All participants in such activities must assume the responsibility for their own actions and safety. The information contained in this guide book cannot replace sound judgment and good decision-making skills, which help reduce the risk exposure; nor does the scope of this book allow for the disclosure of all the potential hazards and risks involved in such activities you participate in. Prepare for the unexpected, and be cautious. The reward will be a safer and more enjoyable experience.

Contents

Preface

In this book, I describe how to use the Global Positioning System as a practical land navigation tool. The emphasis is on GPS as a tool and supplement to classic navigational skills. Remember that GPS is not a substitute for the older land navigation tools: map, compass, and altimeter. Nor is GPS a substitute for common sense or for backcountry experience.

I have avoided technical terms as much as possible; however, jargon and abbreviations do have their uses—it is easier to refer to the direction toward a landmark as a *bearing* than as *the direction toward a landmark*. All terms are explained as they are used. I describe GPS techniques in general terms that apply to any GPS receiver. You should use your receiver's manual alongside this book to learn how to use these techniques with your receiver. Refer to the manufacturers listed in the appendix for up-to-date information on their models. All the manufacturers have websites on the Internet where you can browse through complete specifications and sometimes download equipment manuals.

For those who want to go deeper into global positioning, I have included an advanced GPS section and a further reading list in the appendix. Again, my purpose is to give you an understanding of practical backcountry GPS navigation without getting into unnecessary technical details.

Acknowledgments

I would like to thank longtime friend Jean Rukkila for yet another fine job of proofreading—this time at the last minute. Thanks also to Art Pundt, Coconino County Search and Rescue, and Lee Dexter, Northern Arizona University, for their valuable comments. Moreover, special thanks to Duart Martin, who got me started with GPS and then supported this project through its numerous twists and turns. Again, thanks to all the people at Falcon Publishing.

Introduction

Halfway into an early spring cross-country ski trip on a high plateau, a sudden mountain storm blots out the sun, the wind picks up, and snowflakes fall steadily. You and your group are in a whiteout. Visibility is only a couple of hundred yards, and blowing snow obscures the horizon. Your ski tracks, shallow to begin with, soon disappear in the drifting snow.

You have a map and compass, as always, so you know you can use classic route-finding techniques to find your vehicle. To do this, you would use the map to decide what direction to go, then maintain direction by compass. Once at the edge of the plateau, you could follow it to the road, and then follow the road to your car. However, the irregular edge of the plateau and the road would add a lot of distance to your trip back.

There is a better way. You get your Global Positioning System (GPS) receiver from your pack and turn it on. Within a minute, unaffected by cloud cover or the falling snow, your GPS receiver locks onto the navigation satellites and displays your present position, which you save in the receiver. Using your map, you enter the position of your vehicle in the GPS receiver. Finally, you set up a route using the two saved positions. Now the receiver tells you the direction and distance to your vehicle. You turn the receiver off but put it in a pocket so it is handy. You use your compass to maintain direction as the group sets off. Frequently, you stop and check your progress by turning on the GPS receiver. The map display shows the direction and distance to your car, and it gives a graphic picture of your location and desired course. With the receiver showing your car a half-mile away, you leave the receiver on—although it is awkward to ski with— because you know it would be easy to miss the end of the road in the low visibility. As you ski, the GPS display tells you your speed, direction of travel, and estimated time of arrival, as well as distance and direction to your car. Within a few minutes, the receiver's arrival alarm starts to beep and the lead skier spots your vehicle.

What Is GPS?

The Global Positioning System (GPS) is a system of 21 operational satellites and three non-operational spare satellites orbiting 12,000 miles above the earth. The satellite orbits are arranged so that several satellites are always in view from any point on earth. Spare satellites and ground control stations make up the rest of the system. Though the U.S. Department of Defense developed the system for military use, it is government policy that GPS will be available to all users without charge. Already, GPS is used by businesses to track parcel delivery trucks, by individual motorists to find their way to a specific street address, and by ships and aircraft of all sizes.

The focus of this book is on handheld GPS receivers intended for civilian use, which are suitable for navigation in the backcountry and in self-propelled sports. An expanding variety of GPS receivers is being manufactured. There are large receivers intended to be mounted permanently in vehicles, tiny ones designed to be imbedded in other devices, and credit card-sized receivers designed to plug into data-gathering computers. Specialty receivers are made for marine use, aviation, surveying, and the earth sciences, as well as for the military.

As the name implies, GPS allows the user to determine

position. GPS is unique among the various methods of navigation in that it can determine position very rapidly, with a high degree of accuracy, in any weather and at any time of day, anywhere on our planet. Using radio signals transmitted by the satellites, a GPS receiver can determine position to within 330 feet (100 meters). Small, lightweight, inexpensive handheld receivers are available that make GPS a practical means of backcountry navigation. Because the GPS receiver measures position so often, it can calculate your direction and rate of travel. It can also tell you the direction to travel to reach your destination and display this information on a moving map.

Satellite navigation is not magical. Several real limitations exist. The receiver must have a clear view of the sky in order to receive signals from the satellites. The microwave radio signals travel in a straight line, like light waves, so trees can block the signals, as can high canyon walls. Clouds, rain, and snow do not interfere with the satellite signals. Rarely, poor satellite locations can make it impossible to get a position fix. A GPS receiver is a complex piece of equipment that can fail or be broken, and its batteries can die. In addition, of course, the receiver is only as good as its user.

GPS must be used with the older navigation tools. The position display on a GPS receiver is only a meaningless string of numbers without a map to plot your location. Although some GPS receivers do feature moving maps, the level of detail is just enough for general orientation. Knowing the direction to a favorite spot does not help unless you have a compass to point you in that direction. In addition, a sensitive, temperature-compensated altimeter can read altitude more accurately than a handheld GPS.

HOW GPS WORKS

The heart of GPS is exact measurement of time. Each satellite carries several atomic clocks on board. The satellites transmit precisely timed radio signals, which are picked up by your GPS receiver. The signal carries this information, telling the receiver exactly when the signal left the satellite. Using an onboard computer, the receiver measures time in transit—the time required for the radio signal to travel from the satellite to the receiver. The satellites also transmit a navigation signal giving their exact position. Using this information, your receiver can calculate its exact distance from the satellite and place your receiver somewhere on a spherical surface. When your receiver links up with two more satellites and computes its distance from them, the receiver now knows that it is located on the surface of three imaginary spheres. The point where those spheres intersect is the receiver's position. Acquiring a fourth satellite refines the position calculation so that altitude can be computed.

The GPS satellites in orbit require constant updates transmitted from ground control stations. The ground stations continuously track the satellites and calculate updated positions. Corrections are also made for the drift of the atomic clocks. This information is uplinked to the satellites to update the navigation signal. Without this constant updating, the accuracy of the system would degrade in a matter of days. The ground stations can also reposition satellites and replace them with orbital spares as necessary.

For the backcountry user, GPS is a system of satellite navigation that allows you to accurately find your position with a small, lightweight receiver. With the aid of a map and compass, this breakthrough in navigational capability can take you anyplace you desire.

Navigation Tools

GPS RECEIVERS

A GPS receiver is a sensitive microwave radio receiver combined with a sophisticated computer. Control buttons and a display screen complete the receiver. The technical specifications can be a bit intimidating. It is somewhat difficult to compare different instruments since they are constantly evolving. The following discussion describes features you should consider when buying a receiver. Most importantly, make sure you thoroughly examine your GPS receiver before you buy it and make sure you can return it.

Size

You will naturally want the **smallest receiver** that has the features you will need. GPS receivers are continually getting smaller and lighter as technology improves. A patent has even been issued for a wristwatch-sized GPS receiver! However, consider that smaller receivers have smaller displays; tiny map and navigation screens can be harder to read. Try to get a look at the screen on a receiver before you buy it.

Weight

Minimal weight is desirable, as long as battery life is adequate. Batteries make up a considerable portion of the weight of a GPS receiver. Weights range from less than 8 ounces to over a pound.

Batteries

Battery life varies from as little as four hours to as much as 24 hours or more of continuous use in handheld receivers, using two to four AA size alkaline cells. These figures do not sound practical for extended backcountry trips until you realize that typically the receiver is only on for a few minutes each hour. Even a receiver with four-hour battery life will last for days in the field. Some receivers also have a battery-saving mode in which position updates occur at a slower-than-normal rate. GPS receivers normally use alkaline batteries, but you may be able to use other types of batteries. Lithium batteries are lighter than alkaline batteries, last longer, and work better in cold weather. Rechargeable alkaline or nickel-cadmium batteries save money but do not last as long per charge as throwaway alkaline and lithium batteries.

Consider an **external power connector**; it allows you to use power from a vehicle or external power pack, which saves the receiver's batteries. Make certain that the receiver input voltage range matches the voltage of the power source. You will probably have to buy a power cable from the manufacturer or a third-party supplier, unless the receiver comes with one.

Waterproofing

Since your GPS receiver will be used in bad weather as well as good, look for some degree of **weatherproofing**. Some receivers are sealed and completely waterproof; others are merely water resistant. Sea kayakers and other boaters should get a completely waterproof receiver. There are waterproof dry bags designed for GPS receivers that have attachment points and keep the receiver afloat.

Temperature Limits

All electronic devices have **minimum and maximum temperature limits**, beyond which the device may not function. On GPS receivers, the display in particular may not work in very hot or cold conditions. If you plan to operate in extreme conditions (in deserts in summer or in mountains in winter, for example), make certain your GPS receiver can handle it. For cold weather use, make sure your receiver can be operated while wearing gloves. Battery life is shortened by cold temperatures, so you may have to run your receiver from an external battery pack kept warm inside your clothing. Or you can keep the unit inside your clothing.

Accuracy

The Department of Defense limits the **accuracy** available to civilian users; the normal accuracy for civilians is 330 feet horizontally and 512 feet vertically. This is despite all handheld GPS receivers having an inherent horizontal accuracy of 49 feet. However, 330 feet is accurate enough for most backcountry navigation. Positions are displayed to a precision of 3 feet, but do not be fooled into thinking the receiver is that accurate. (See "Advanced GPS" for more on the technical aspects of GPS accuracy.) Some receivers have a position-averaging feature, which uses a series of position fixes over time, and claim accuracy of better than 50 feet horizontally.

Channels

Receiver channels refer to the number of satellites from which the receiver can receive information. The GPS receiver must pick up signals from at least three satellites to determine position and four satellites to calculate both position and altitude. Reception from more satellites improves the receiver's accuracy and allows the receiver a better chance of maintaining a lock when satellites are temporarily blocked from view. (A receiver is locked when it is receiving signals from enough satellites to produce a reliable position.) Eight channels should be the minimum on your receiver—most receivers receive 12 channels. Older GPS receivers use a single receiver channel to pick up signals from multiple satellites by scanning four or more satellites in turn, a technique called multiplexing. Since the signals are not received continuously, it is easier for the receiver to lose lock on a satellite. Newer instruments have separate receivers for up to 12 parallel channels. Each channel continuously receives signals from a single satellite. A parallel channel receiver locks on more quickly than a multiplexing receiver and maintains that lock better under varying conditions, such as a partially obstructed sky or rapid changes in direction and speed. Since parallel channel receivers have become inexpensive, avoid multiplexed receivers.

Antennas

Two types of **antennas** are used on handheld GPS receivers: quadrifilar and patch. The quadrifilar is a coil of wire in a rectangular plastic housing, forming a hornlike projection on the top or side of the receiver. Quadrifilar antennas are better at receiving from satellites close to the horizon, but are poor at picking up satellite signals from directly overhead. Patch antennas are flat and are built into the top of the receiver. They are better at picking out satellites overhead, but poorer at seeing satellites less than 10 degrees above the horizon. Either type may be fixed—meaning you have to move the entire receiver to reorient the antenna—or movable—meaning the antenna can be repositioned independently of the receiver. Movable antennas are more versatile in getting fixes in bad locations, but they are bulkier. Quadrifilar antennas are often removable so that they can be mounted on the inside of your vehicle's windshield for better reception. The connecting cable must be kept short because the satellite signals are very weak and get lost in long cables. If you need to mount a GPS antenna farther than a few feet from the receiver, you will have to use an amplified antenna, which strengthens the satellite signals before sending them down the cable.

Measurement Units

Some receivers allow you to change only the overall **measurement unit system**. Others allow individual displays to be customized. For example, you could display distance in nautical miles and elevation in meters. If you have special requirements, be sure your receiver can be set to use the units you will need.

Coordinate Systems

The GPS receiver displays your position using coordinates, which is a set of numbers used to accurately specify location. Your receiver must be capable of displaying position using the **coordinate system** used by your map. At a minimum, the receiver should use the latitude/longitude and Universal Transverse Mercator coordinate systems. Other coordinate systems may be required in different parts of the world. Make certain your receiver can use the coordinate system you will need.

Map Datums

All American-made GPS receivers have the **map datums** used in North America; if you plan to use your receiver in other countries, make sure it has the appropriate datums. Maps are being converted to WGS84 (World Geodetic Standard 1984, the GPS mapping standard) worldwide, but this process will take some time.

Waypoint Capability

Most GPS receivers can store 100 or more **waypoints**. A waypoint is a location described with coordinates and used for GPS navigation. Some receivers use the term "landmark" instead of waypoint, but landmark more correctly refers to a physical location on the ground that is identified by a feature, such as a trail intersection or a mountain peak. All receivers identify waypoints with short descriptive names made up of five or six characters and numbers. Some receivers will let you describe waypoints with a longer phrase. In either case, you will probably want to keep separate notes describing the purpose of your waypoints. A typical GPS receiver can store five or more routes, each containing 20 or more waypoints. Since it is rarely possible to travel in a straight line in the backcountry, for practical use a GPS receiver should be capable of handling routes with at least a dozen waypoints.

Track Logging

Consider the **track-logging** feature; it allows you to record your actual route as you travel. The receiver does this by automatically storing position fixes in memory, either at preset time intervals or when you make changes in direction or speed. The length of the track log record is limited by the amount of memory in the receiver—when the memory is full, the oldest track fixes are erased. Most receivers display your track on their plot screen. Track logging is useful for comparing your actual route of travel with the desired route. In addition, many GPS receivers allow you to convert the track log into a route so that you can use it to backtrack or return to your starting point. With suitable software, some receivers allow you to copy the track log to a computer for mapping and other purposes. **Caution:** Track logging can be very useful when you are exploring back roads in a vehicle, where external power is available for the receiver. The feature is not as useful for hiking or other self-propelled activities because the receiver must be left on to record the track, which uses up your batteries.

Memory

The **memory** in a GPS receiver retains user-defined waypoint and route information, as well as various settings such as those for distance and speed units. The more memory the receiver has, the more waypoint and route information it can hold. Check that the receiver has a backup system that maintains the memory long enough to change batteries—if it doesn't, you will lose all your stored waypoints and custom settings.

Speed Limits

A few manufacturers purposely design **speed limits** into their products. For example, one company makes receivers intended for ground navigation and another line of receivers intended for aircraft navigation. To prevent the ground receivers from being used for air navigation, GPS ground receivers are programmed to stop working above 114 miles per hour. If you are a pilot who would like to use the same GPS receiver in your plane and on the ground, either make sure the receiver does not have a speed limitation or buy a receiver intended for air navigation.

Database Capability

Receivers that are more expensive have a **built-in database**. A database is a list of permanent waypoints. Aviation receivers, for example, usually have databases containing waypoints for airports. You can pick your destination by its name, which saves you the trouble of manually entering the coordinates. Since backcountry users have so many possible destinations, GPS receivers intended for ground uses do not usually have databases.

Plot Screen

Nearly all GPS receivers have a **plot screen** that shows your position in relation to nearby waypoints. You should be able to set the plot screen to both north up (the top of the screen is always north) and track up (the top of the screen points toward your direction of travel). You should also be able to zoom in and out, to change the area and amount of detail the plot shows, and to pan the plot to show different areas. Some receivers feature autozoom, which increases the scale of the plot screen as you get closer to a waypoint. Usually, plot screens allow you to enter a new waypoint from a position marker on the screen or to navigate directly to a position selected from the screen.

Area Maps

More sophisticated receivers have graphics capable of show-ing a map of your surrounding area. This allows the receiver to display a **moving map**, which changes as you move, to graphically present your position and direction of travel in relation to surrounding features. Detail shown may include cities, highways, city streets, back roads, rivers, and coastlines. Some receivers allow you to load your own maps from a computer. Even the most detailed moving maps are no substitute for a large-scale topographic map in the backcountry. However, a moving map is very useful for general navigation, especially in a vehicle, boat, or aircraft. Because it shows your position in relation to surrounding highways and towns, a GPS receiver with a moving map can help you navigate out of the wilderness in an emergency. In the future, as electronic memory becomes cheaper, GPS maps will be able to show more detail.

Displays

Almost all handheld GPS receivers have **liquid crystal display** (LCD) screens, but they vary in quality and readability. The display uses tiny dots called pixels; the more pixels, the more information that can be displayed. Make sure that navigation information is displayed in large, readable characters. Check that the display is readable in dim light as well as in bright sunlight (a contrast setting allows you to adjust the display for different light levels). Most receivers have backlit displays that can be turned off to save batteries, or set to come on for a few seconds when you press a key.

Sunrise and Sunset

Many GPS receivers will display **sunrise and sunset data**, and in some cases moon phases and sun azimuth/elevation, for any waypoint or location, on any date and at any time. This information can be useful for trip planning and for outdoor photography.

Simulator Mode

Simulator mode capability allows you to simulate navigation when you are not actually moving. You can manually enter a starting position, heading (your direction of travel), and speed. It is a great way to learn how to use your receiver, but make certain the display clearly indicates when the receiver is in simulator mode.

Data Port

A **data port** is a connection point on the receiver that allows you to connect the receiver with other devices to send and receive data. You can connect your receiver to a personal computer to enter and maintain more waypoints and routes than the receiver's memory can hold, and you can also use such applications as moving maps and other mapping software.

Accessories

Most receivers come with basic **accessories** such as a carrying case. Optional accessories usually include an external power cord and an external antenna or antenna extension cable. Other accessories include mounting kits and computer interface kits. You may find a mounting kit useful if you plan to use your receiver in a vehicle often. A computer interface kit allows you to transfer data such as waypoints to and from a computer.

Controls

Handheld receivers have a limited amount of space so designers use as few **control buttons** as possible. Many receivers use four buttons to move up, down, right, and left through the main pages. A page on a GPS receiver is a screen of information. All of the most commonly used navigation and input pages should be readily accessible. Using up and down buttons to scroll through the alphabet is how you enter characters and numbers. Functions used less frequently, such as datum and coordinate settings, are usually found on a menu page. The best way to decide if you like the controls on a receiver is to try them before buying it. An important item to check is the method used to turn the power on and off. It should be difficult to turn the receiver on or off accidentally. Most receivers have a recessed power switch or button.

Accuracy Warning System

A critical feature is the **warning system,** used to tell you if navigational accuracy is degraded due to poor satellite reception, or to warn you of problems with the receiver itself. Some receivers use icons on the screen as warnings; others beep and display a message.

Flexibility

User-changeable fields are available on some receivers. These let you customize the navigation screens to show exactly the data you need. However, all receivers display the important navigation information.

Odometer

Most receivers have an **odometer** display that works the same way the settable odometer does in your car: it accumulates distance from the last time it was reset. The odometer function is most useful in air or water navigation, when you are traveling in straight lines. On roads or trails, the odometer reads lower than your actual travel distance. Also, the odometer only works if the unit is left on all the time.

MAPS FOR GPS

A map for GPS navigation must have a coordinate system that allows you to specify locations accurately. The coordinate system is essential for finding your position on the map from the GPS position readout, and for converting landmarks on the map into waypoints in the receiver.

Maps are produced with varying amounts of detail and coverage. **Scale** is the ratio of distance on the map to distance on the ground and is the most common way of expressing the amount of detail on a map. For example, a map with a scale of 1:5,000,000 means that 1 inch on the map represents 5,000,000 inches—or about 80 miles—on the ground. A map with a scale of 1:24,000 means that 1 inch on the map represents 24,000 inches, or 2,000 feet, on the ground. Obviously, the 1:24,000 map can show greater detail than the 1:5,000,000 map, but it covers less area. A map of the United States on a scale of 1:5,000,000 will comfortably fit on a wall but does not have nearly enough detail for backcountry use. On the other hand, the 1:24,000 map shows plenty of detail for land navigation on foot, but covers a very small area of about 7 by 9 miles.

USGS topographic maps are the most accurate maps published in the United States. A topographic map uses **contour lines** to show elevation and the shape of the land. A contour line is simply a line that represents the same elevation everywhere on the map. Topo maps come in various scales; the 7.5-minute series is the largest scale map and has the most detail. These maps cover an area of about 63 square miles at a scale of 1:24,000. Most developed nations have a similar series of topographic maps, though at different scales.

The USDA Forest Service, the Bureau of Land Management (BLM), and other land management agencies also publish maps useful for backcountry navigation. The most commonly available maps are visitor maps, usually printed at a scale of 1:126,720, or 0.5-inch to the mile. These usually cover a major portion of a national forest or other land management area. Newer visitor maps are topographic, but most of the maps in print are still planimetric, which means they do not show elevations and are basically road maps. Because they show the official agency road network, including road numbers, they are very useful for finding your way to the trailhead. Lat/long is usually the primary coordinate system on these maps. Positions can be measured to within 0.1 mile or so, which is accurate enough to specify the location of a trailhead or road intersection in your GPS receiver.

Several companies produce private recreational maps. These vary in scale and accuracy but often are more up to date on roads, trails, and recreational facilities than government maps. Some do not have coordinate systems, however. (See Appendix for information on obtaining maps.)

UNIVERSAL TRANSVERSE MERCATOR (UTM) GRID AND LATITUDE/LONGITUDE READERS

Although not essential, a UTM grid reader (also called a roamer) makes it easier to determine waypoints on a map. If you prefer to work with latitude and longitude (lat/long), a lat/long reader is useful. You must use a UTM grid reader or lat/long reader designed for the scale of map you are working with. Most readers work with several different scales. Both types are printed on clear plastic, and may be combined on one reader. (An example is Topo Companion, which has UTM and lat/long readers for all the USGS topographic map scales. See Appendix for ordering sources.)

COMPASSES

A good compass is essential for backcountry navigation. Since compasses point to magnetic north and maps use true north, it is useful to have a compass that can be adjusted for declination. Better compasses have a small screw or other adjustment that lets you dial in the declination, essentially converting the compass to a true-north device. Because the amount of declination varies from place to place, you must reset the compass before heading to a new area. An orienteering-style compass with a clear plastic baseplate is also useful, because the compass can be used to lay out bearings on a map, saving the need to carry a separate protractor. Some newer compasses have UTM grid readers on their baseplates.

ALTIMETERS

An accurate temperature-compensated altimeter measures elevation to within 30 feet, which is far more accurate than a GPS receiver. Altimeters are actually barometers that measure atmospheric pressure, and since the pressure changes with the weather, an altimeter must be set to a known elevation every few hours during use. GPS and a large-scale topographic map can be used to set your altimeter: use the GPS to determine your position, then read your elevation from the map. To set your altimeter, always use the elevation from the map, never the GPS readout of elevation.

Navigation Skills

MAP AND COMPASS REVIEW

Learning to read a map is made easier by orienting the map so it is lined up with the terrain. There are three ways to do this: (1) Use a compass to determine north (see below) and turn the map so its north agrees with the compass; (2) if you are on a linear feature such as a road or a trail, turn the map until the same feature on the map is lined up with the real one; or (3) if you can see one or more distant, known landmarks, turn the map until your position and the landmark's position on the map are lined up with the real positioning. Once your map is oriented, you can relate landmark symbols on the map with the actual landmarks in the countryside.

To find your direction or orient your map, you need to know how to use a compass. You will be working with bearings (also called azimuths, tracks, or directions), the direction from one position to another, measured in degrees clockwise from north. North is 000 degrees, east is 090 degrees, south is 180 degrees, and west is 270 degrees. Bearings can be expressed relative to true north or magnetic north. True north is the direction toward the geographic North Pole, the axis about which the earth spins. Magnetic north is the direction a compass needle points when it aligns itself with the earth's geomagnetic field. The difference between magnetic north and true north is called declination. Declination in the 48 United States varies from about 25 degrees east in Washington State to about 20 degrees west in Maine. It changes slowly over time because of changes in the earth's magnetic field. Declination, as of the date of publication, is printed in the margins of USGS maps.

Figure 1:
Declination

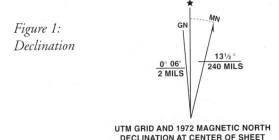

UTM GRID AND 1972 MAGNETIC NORTH
DECLINATION AT CENTER OF SHEET

To convert a true bearing to a magnetic bearing, subtract east declination or add west declination. Reverse this procedure to convert from magnetic to true. Since it is so easy to make a mistake in this process, it is simpler to always work with true bearings because all good maps are printed with true north at the top. Remember to stay well away from iron or steel objects, such as vehicles, when using a compass. The larger the mass of metal, the farther the distance you should be from it. For example, you should stand 50 feet from a car or truck and 3 feet from a small object such as a pocketknife.

GPS SETTINGS

There are a number of settings you should make in your GPS receiver before using it in the field. These settings are usually found under a setup menu.

Most GPS receivers allow you several different **mode choices**, including simulator, battery saver, and normal. Simulator mode (also termed "demo" mode on some receivers) will not pick up any satellites or positions and is only useful for practicing at home. You do not want to be in simulator mode if you are trying to navigate in the field. Battery-saver mode is the best for backpacking or other extended trips where there are no power sources along the way. Normal mode is usually necessary for track logging and backtrack features and should be your choice if you are not worried about conserving batteries.

A bonus of carrying a GPS receiver is the availability of accurate time. While it is on, the receiver synchronizes its clock with the accurate clocks on the satellites. Known technically as **GPS time**, the time shown on the receiver is within a few seconds of the world standard time, Universal Time Coordinated (UTC). On most receivers, you can change the displayed time to your local time zone by determining the offset from UTC for your time zone. Check your receiver's manual for specific instructions.

You also need to make sure your receiver is set to the proper **units of measurement**. Most receivers can be set to statute, nautical, or metric units. Some receivers allow you to change only the overall unit system. Normally, because statute miles (MI or SM on your screen) are the standard units of distance on land in the United States, you will use statute units for backcountry navigation. (Unqualified references to "miles" always mean statute miles.) Nautical miles ("nm" on your screen) are slightly longer than statute miles and are used primarily for sea and air navigation. If you sea kayak, you will be using coastal marine charts and you will want to set your receiver to nautical miles. Most other countries use kilometers (KM on your screen) for land navigation, so you will need to set your receiver to metric units abroad.

You can set the GPS receiver to use either **true north** or **magnetic north**, but for land navigation using topographic maps, true north is easier to use. You also may have several options for setting your **screen orientation**. Most GPS receivers have options that include north up and track. North up is the most useful for navigating in the backcountry because the screen orientation is always the same.

Every map that is accurate enough for navigation is based on horizontal and vertical **map datums**. A datum is a model of the earth's surface based on a surveyed network of physical points. In North America, the most common datum is the North American Datum of 1927 (NAD27), which is used on USGS maps, USDA Forest Service (USDAFS) maps, and many other government and private maps based on these. Other regions of the world have their own datums; there are more than a hundred in use.

.

The GPS receiver must be set to the same datum used by your map; otherwise, position errors will result.

The receiver always stores positions internally based on the WGS84 datum and converts positions to the user-selected datum for display. If the wrong datum is selected, the displayed position can be off by as much as a mile. Before starting to work with maps, set the correct datum in your receiver. The datum should be printed in the margin of the map. If the datum is not printed on the map, it is probably safe to use NAD27 in North America. Your receiver may break NAD27 into separate datums for the continental United States (CONUS), Alaska, Canada, etc. In this case, select NAD27 CONUS if you are in the lower 48 states. Most recreational maps are based on USGS maps, so they use NAD27. Aeronautical charts and some newer maps use WGS84. Outside North America, there are many local datums and setting the wrong datum may result in large errors. Gradually, all maps are being converted to WGS84, but this will take many years.

You must set the GPS receiver to the **coordinate system** used by your map before entering waypoints or plotting GPS positions on the map. Fortunately, there are just two common systems in North America: Universal Transverse Mercator (UTM) and latitude/longitude (lat/long). UTM tends to be easier to work with, but lat/long is more universal. For most backcountry trips, UTM is probably your best choice for a coordinate system.

BRUCE'S DEFAULT GPS RECEIVER SETTINGS	
Mode	Normal or battery saver if available
Time	Local time
Units of Measurement	Miles (MI or SM)
True or Magnetic North	True North
Screen Orientation	North up
Map Datums	NAD27
Coordinate System	UTM

LATITUDE AND LONGITUDE

The most universal coordinate system is **latitude and longitude (lat/long)**, which can be used to describe positions anywhere on earth. Latitude is the distance north or south of the equator measured in degrees from 0 to 90, with 0 at the equator and 90 north at the North Pole. Longitude is the distance east or west of the prime meridian, measured in degrees. The prime meridian is located in Greenwich, England. A degree is 1/360th of a circle; in this case, the circle is the circumference of the earth. Latitude and longitude are usually expressed in degrees, minutes, and seconds. A minute is 1/60th of a degree, and a second is 1/60th of a minute.

For example, the airport at Helena, Montana is located at 46 degrees 36 seconds 24 minutes north latitude, and 111 degrees 58 minutes 54 seconds west longitude. This position is written as N46° 36' 24" W111° 58' 54". Decimal minutes

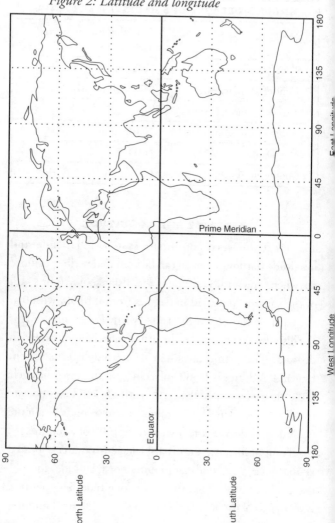

Figure 2: Latitude and longitude

can be used instead of seconds; the same position would then read N46° 36.14' W111° 58.90'. Rarely, decimal degrees are used: N46.6000° W111.9900°. Most GPS receivers can be set to display positions in any of these formats.

Although lat/long is found on nearly all good maps, it can be difficult to work with. On some maps, including USGS topographic maps, it is awkward to interpret between the lat/long tick marks. Although a minute of latitude is the same distance (1 nautical mile) anywhere on earth, the same is not true of longitude. As you move away from the equator toward either pole, the meridians converge and a minute of longitude covers less distance on the ground. In addition, working with the lat/long system is easier if you use a special latitude/longitude reader. Otherwise, you will have to eyeball the coordinates, which can be good enough (see the discussion of determining coordinates below).

UNIVERSAL TRANSVERSE MERCATOR (UTM)

Universal Transverse Mercator (UTM) is a more useful coordinate system for land navigation. UTM uses distances from standard reference points to grid maps into 1000 meter intervals (1000 meters = 1 kilometer = 0.62 miles). These squares remain the same at all latitudes covered by the system, so it is easy to read positions on the map. UTM breaks the world up into 60 zones, each of which is 6 degrees east to west, then specifies position in meters north of the equator and east from the prime **meridian** of the zone. (A meridian is a north-south line of reference.) The position of the prime meridian is defined as 500,000 meters east (called the "false easting") to start with, so that all coordinates have positive numbers. A zone letter is used to break the zones into 8-degree north-south blocks of latitude but is not necessary to specify position. For example, to specify the location of the Helena airport to the nearest meter (3.3 feet), you would use the coordinates 12 424802mE 5161726mN. The "12" is the zone, "424802" is the **easting** (to the right on your map), and "5161726" is the **northing** (up on your map). This means that the airport is located 424,802 meters east of the zone 12 reference meridian and 5,161,726 meters north of the equator. Any desired level of precision can be used. If you want to specify the location of the Helena airport only to the nearest 1000 meters, drop the last three digits of the easting and northing, and write the position as 12 424 5161.

UTM does not cover the entire planet; it stops at 84° north and 80° south. Polar explorers use the Universal Polar Stereographic grid system. Because the 1000-meter grids are squares overlaid on the curved surface of the earth, the grid lines are not exactly aligned with true north except at the prime meridian. The discrepancy can be several degrees. The difference from true north is called grid declination and is printed in the margin of USGS maps. *Do not use UTM grid lines as true north reference lines unless you correct for grid declination.*

Lat/long and UTM references are included in the margins of USGS maps. Some USGS maps are overlaid with a

Figure 3: UTM grid zones for the United States

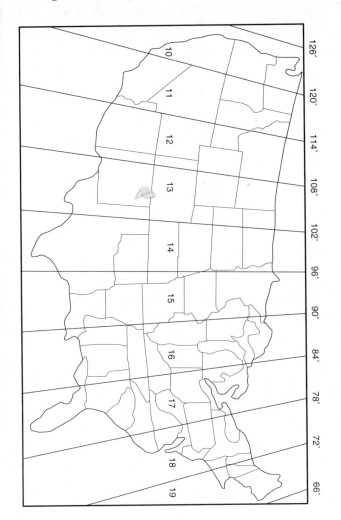

light gray UTM grid in 1000-meter intervals. Unlike lat/long, the UTM grid does not change with latitude, so it is easy to measure positions on the map. A UTM grid reader or any convenient straightedge, such as another map, can be used to measure position down to 10 meters on a large-scale map.

There are many other grid systems used in different parts of the world. For example, topographic maps in Great Britain use the British Grid, and Swiss maps use the Swiss Grid. These systems are metric grids similar to the UTM grid, but with different origin points. Luckily, the same UTM principles apply to all metric grid systems.

Finding Waypoints

To describe the location of landmarks (trailhead, trail junction, creek crossing, mountaintop, etc.) in terms that a GPS receiver can use, we create a waypoint. A waypoint is a set of numbers that describes a unique position (on the ground and on the map), which you enter into the receiver and give a unique name.

In GPS, as well as in other forms of electronic navigation, waypoints are specified in terms of coordinates, and can be located anywhere. Normally a waypoint is created by reading the coordinates from a map or by saving your current location in the receiver, but a waypoint can be specified relative to another waypoint or obtained from a guidebook, a friend, or other source.

When we combine more than one waypoint, we determine a route. A route is simply a path between two waypoints. Starting and ending waypoints can be used to define a route, a stored plan of travel. Additional waypoints can be used to define turning points or intermediate goals along the route.

PREPARING YOUR MAPS

Whether you plan to work with UTM or lat/long, it helps to prepare maps at home. Either for trip planning or in the field, there are a few steps you can take to make it easier to use coordinates. Some USGS maps, for example, do not have UTM grids overlaid on the map—only tick marks in the margins. Pregridding the map makes using UTM easier.

Pregridding a USGS Map with UTM Grids

Use a long ruler to carefully draw a grid on the map, connecting the UTM tick marks. On 7.5-minute topographic maps these are the blue tick marks spaced 1000 meters (1 kilometer) apart. Use a pencil or fine point, waterproof pen, and draw the lines lightly so that you do not cover any important information on the map.

Pregridding a USGS Map with Lat/Long Grids

Use a long ruler to carefully draw in the meridians and parallels between the lat/long margin tick marks. You can locate the lat/long tick marks by looking for minutes and seconds, for example, 47'30". On the USGS 7.5-minute maps, there are tick marks every 2.5 minutes, so you will end up with two parallels and two meridians, dividing the map into nine blocks.

FINDING A WAYPOINT WITH UTM GRID AND UTM GRID READER

1. Make sure you are using the correct grid reader for the map scale. For this example, we will determine the UTM coordinates of Aspen Spring on the Dane Canyon, Arizona 7.5-minute USGS topographic map.
2. Place the zero point (the upper right corner) of the UTM grid reader on Aspen Spring.

3. Align the scales on the grid reader with the grid lines on the map.

4. Read 260 meters (to the right) along the top scale of the UTM grid reader at the nearest 1000-meter grid line to the west.

5. Append 260 meters to the 1000-meter grid number, which is 482, to get 482260, the easting.

6. Next, read 120 meters north (up) where the scale on the right side crosses the nearest 1000-meter grid line to the south, which is the 3816 grid line.

7. Append 120 meters to 3816 to get 3816120, which is the northing.

8. Finally, refer to the bottom left edge of the map to get UTM Zone 12. The full UTM coordinate for Aspen Spring is 12 482260mE 3816120mN. The "mE" and "mN" are not entered into the receiver, so on the display these coordinates would read 12 S 482260 3816120. (The "S" is the zone letter, which the receiver calculates from the northing. You do not need to enter it yourself. Note that the 1,000s and 10,000s digits [**82** and **16**] are written in bold, or larger numbers, to make the coordinate easier to read.)

9. Now, enter the waypoint into your receiver. On most receivers, this is done by going to the waypoint page or by picking the waypoint list from a menu. The waypoint page may have a "new" function, which when selected, presents a blank waypoint. Enter the waypoint name by using the up and down arrow keys to select the letter or number and use the left/right arrow keys to move to other character positions. The coordinates are entered the same way. Call this waypoint ASPEN.

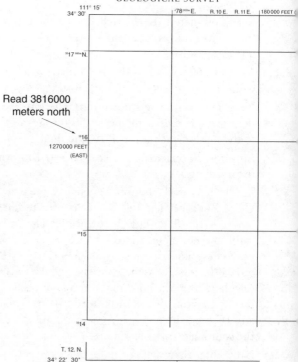

UNITED STATES
DEPARTMENT OF THE INTERIOR
GEOLOGICAL SURVEY

(LONG VALLEY)
3753 III SE

111° 15'
34° 30'

'78⁰⁰⁰ᵐ E.   R. 10 E.   R. 11 E.   180 000 FEET

³⁸17⁰⁰⁰ᵐ N.

Read 3816000
meters north

³⁸16
1 270 000 FEET
(EAST)

³⁸15

³⁸14

T. 12. N.
34° 22' 30°
111° 15'   '78

(PAYSON NORTH)
3762 IV SE

Read Zone 12

Mapped by the U. S. Forest Service
Edited and published by the Geological Survey
Control by USGS, USC&GS and USFS
Topography by photogrammetric methods from aerial
photography taken 1965. Field checked by USGS 1972
Projection: Arizona coordinate system, central zone
(transverse Mercator)
10,000-foot grid ticks based on Arizona coordinate
system, central and east zones
1000-meter Universal Transverse Mercator grid ticks
zone 12, shown in blue. 1927 North American datum
To place on the predicted North American datum 1983
move the projection lines 63 meters east as shown by
dashed corner ticks
there may be private inholdings within the boundaries of
the national or State reservations shown on this map
Where omitted, land lines have not been established

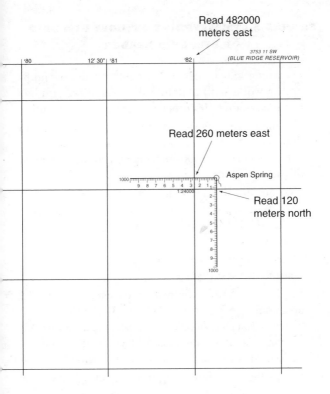

Read 482000
meters east

3753 11 SW
(BLUE RIDGE RESERVOIR)

'80   12' 30" | '81   '82 |

Read 260 meters east

Aspen Spring

1000   9 8 7 6 5 4 3 2 1
1:24000

Read 120
meters north

2
3
4
5
6
7
8
9
1000

(map detail deleted for clarity)

*Figure 4: Locating Aspen Spring with a UTM grid reader
and gridded USGS 7.5-minute topographic map*

FINDING A UTM WAYPOINT WITHOUT UTM GRID OR UTM GRID READER

1. Use a long straightedge (in the field, the edge of another map works well) to draw a short section of grid line from the nearest 1000-meter tick marks to the south.

2. Use the nearest 1000-meter tick marks to the west to draw another short section of grid line. (The idea is to define the nearest 1000-meter corner to the southwest of your waypoint.)

3. Use your straightedge to draw your waypoint to the top or bottom edge of the map. Keep the straightedge parallel to the UTM grid by observing the tick marks on both margins.

4. Measure the distance in meters to the nearest UTM tick mark to the west (left).

5. USGS maps have a kilometer and meter scale printed on the margin that you could read to the nearest 100 meters. Use a piece of paper to transfer the distance from the map margin to the scale. Add this figure to the value printed at the tick mark to get the easting.

6. Repeat the procedure using the left and right margins to get the northing.

7. Enter the waypoint into your GPS receiver.

Whatever method you use, read UTM coordinates to the nearest 10 meters when working with a 7.5-minute map. Although your receiver is accurate to only 100 meters, GPS errors are cumulative, so you want to minimize any source of errors. In addition, GPS receivers will become more accurate in the future.

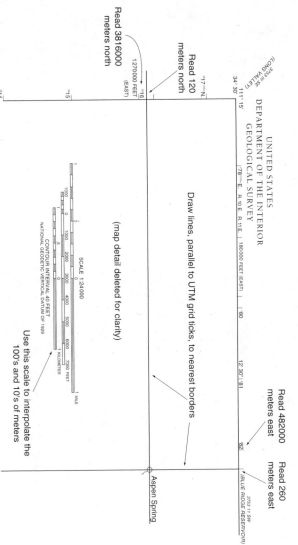

Figure 5: Determining a UTM waypoint without UTM grid reader and an ungridded map

Read 3816000 meters north

Read 120 meters north

1270000 FEET (EAST)

3753 III SE (LONG VALLEY)

34° 30′

111° 15′

78000m.E. R. 10 E. R. 11 E. 180000 FEET (EAST)

'80

12′ 30″ '81

Read 482000 meters east

Read 260 meters east

3753 II SW (BLUE RIDGE RESERVOIR)

'82

Draw lines, parallel to UTM grid ticks, to nearest borders

(map detail deleted for clarity)

UNITED STATES
DEPARTMENT OF THE INTERIOR
GEOLOGICAL SURVEY

SCALE 1:24 000

1000   0   1000   2000   3000   4000   5000   6000   7000 FEET

1   .5   0   1 KILOMETER

1   .5   0   1 MILE

CONTOUR INTERVAL 40 FEET
NATIONAL GEODETIC VERTICAL DATUM OF 1929

Aspen Spring

Use this scale to interpolate the 100's and 10's of meters

34° 30″ N.

'17000m.N.

'16

'15

'14

45

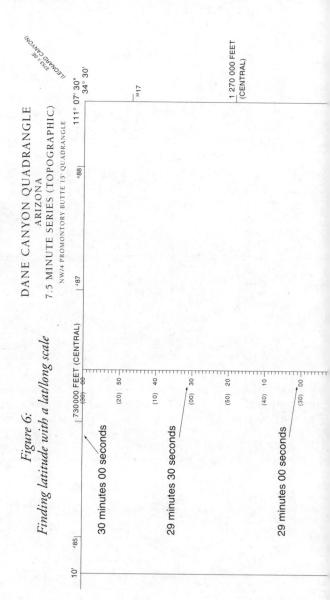

Figure 6:
Finding latitude with a lat/long scale

DANE CANYON QUADRANGLE
ARIZONA
7.5 MINUTE SERIES (TOPOGRAPHIC)
NW/4 PROMONTORY BUTTE 15' QUADRANGLE

30 minutes 00 seconds

29 minutes 30 seconds

29 minutes 00 seconds

46

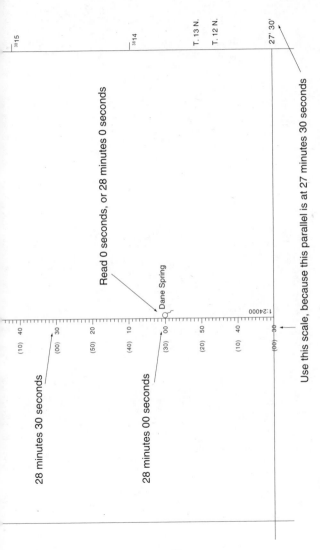

38°15

38°14

T. 13 N.

T. 12 N.

27' 30'

Read 0 seconds, or 28 minutes 0 seconds

Dane Spring

Use this scale, because this parallel is at 27 minutes 30 seconds

1:24000

(10) 40
(00) 30
(50) 20
(40) 10
(30) 00
(20) 50
(10) 40
(00) 30

28 minutes 30 seconds

28 minutes 00 seconds

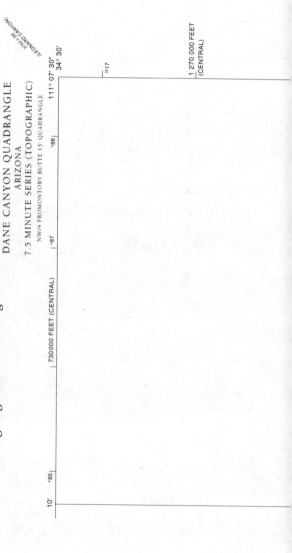

Figure 7:
Finding longitude with lat/long scale

DANE CANYON QUADRANGLE
ARIZONA
7.5 MINUTE SERIES (TOPOGRAPHIC)
NW/4 PROMONTORY BUTTE 15' QUADRANGLE

(LEONARD CANYON)
3764 II SE

111° 07' 30"
34° 30'

'88

'87

730000 FEET (CENTRAL)

'85

10'

³⁴17

1 270 000 FEET
(CENTRAL)

48

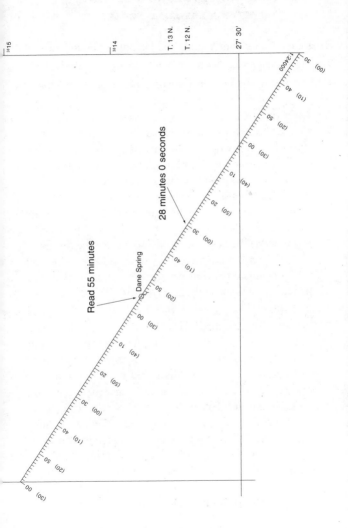

FINDING A LAT/LONG WAYPOINT
WITH A LAT/LONG SCALE

For accurate work with latitude and longitude, you will need a lat/long reader or scale. For this example, we will find the lat/long of Dane Spring on the Dane Canyon Quadrangle in Arizona.

1. Latitude is read using the scale vertically, with the bottom of the scale on the lower parallel of latitude. Notice that there are two sets of numbers on the scale. Since the latitude (and longitude) ticks are 2.5 minutes apart on the 7.5-minute series maps, the bottom of the scale may be on a parallel at 00 or 30 seconds (0.5 minute). If the parallel is at 00 seconds, use the (00) numbers. In this case, the parallel at the bottom of the reader is at 34 degrees 27 minutes 30 seconds, so we use the numbers that start with 30. Read up the scale to Dane Spring at 00. This puts the spring exactly 30 seconds north of the parallel, which makes the latitude N34° 28' 00", or north 34 degrees 28 minutes 00 seconds.

2. Longitude is measured with the base of the scale on the meridian to the right, which in this case is the **neatline** (the edge of the detail area of the map). Because longitude minutes are shorter than latitude minutes on this map, the scale has to lie at a slant so that the top will lie on the next meridian to the left. Move the scale up or down until it crosses your waypoint, then make sure the ends are still on their meridians. Again, because the neatline is at longitude 111 degrees 07 minutes 30 seconds, use the numbers that start with 30. Reading to the left, we pass 00, which is 111 degrees 08 minutes, then read 55 seconds at Dane Spring. This makes the

longitude W111° 08' 55", or west 111 degrees 8 minutes 55 seconds.

3. Your lat/long waypoint is N34° 28' 00" W111° 08' 55".

4. Enter this waypoint into your receiver as DANESP.

DEFINING A WAYPOINT FROM A KNOWN WAYPOINT

You can also define a new waypoint using distance and direction from a waypoint already in the receiver. Using Dane Spring as our known waypoint, we can create a new waypoint at McClintock Spring. For this example, we will use an orienteering compass with a clear baseplate, but you can also use a ruler and a protractor.

1. Put one corner of the compass baseplate at Dane Spring, then align the edge of the baseplate with McClintock Spring.

2. Turn the compass capsule until the north lines are parallel to a meridian or the neatline. Now you can read the true bearing, 352 degrees, at the lubber line next to the scale on the capsule. (The lubber line is the reference mark on the compass where bearings are read.)

3. Now, make sure that either Dane or McClintock Spring is at the zero point on the baseplate scale. In this case, Dane Spring is at 0, so we read 9.2 centimeters at McClintock Spring.

4. Move the compass to the mileage scale at the bottom of the map, and read 1.6 miles at 9.2 cm on the baseplate scale.

5. Define the new waypoint in your GPS receiver by entering the name of the reference waypoint, DANESP, and then the distance and direction. We will call the new waypoint MCCLNT.

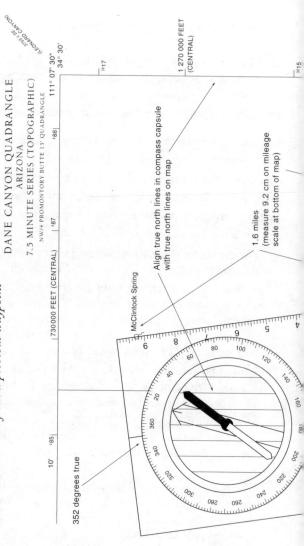

Figure 8: Finding a new waypoint using distance and direction from a previous waypoint

52

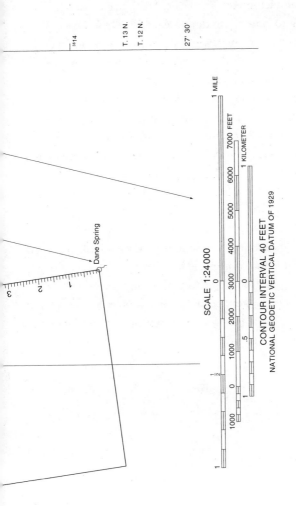

SCALE 1:24 000

CONTOUR INTERVAL 40 FEET
NATIONAL GEODETIC VERTICAL DATUM OF 1929

Dane Spring

T. 13 N.
T. 12 N.

27' 30'

This method can also be used with maps that only have lat/long to simplify finding waypoints. Define a waypoint at a corner of the map where the latitude and longitude are printed, then use this waypoint to find new waypoints using distance and direction.

Keep in mind that in field use, you can often estimate coordinates by estimating the position of a map landmark in relation to the coordinate grid or tick marks. This technique is especially useful in bad weather or when you do not have a UTM grid reader or lat/long scale. It also works well when you know your position via conventional navigation but want to use your GPS receiver to confirm it. You can read the coordinates from the receiver's position screen and estimate their location on your map. Always check that a new waypoint is in a reasonable location by noting its distance and direction from an existing waypoint. Incorrectly entering a digit or two can put a waypoint hundreds or thousands of miles away from its correct location, but it is harder to catch an error of only a mile or so.

Field Technique

When using a GPS receiver in a vehicle, run the GPS receiver on the vehicle's power if possible. Use an external antenna for best results—these usually have suction cups to mount on the inside of the windshield, giving the antenna maximum view of the sky. If you do not have an external antenna, keep the receiver near a window—preferably the front windshield. The newer parallel receivers usually work well without an external antenna. When driving and using a GPS receiver to navigate, it is safest to have a passenger hold the receiver and do the navigation.

If you are hiking, skiing, paddling, or cycling and the receiver is running on its batteries, leave the receiver off except when using it to find your position and to navigate. Use the battery-saving mode if your receiver has one. Avoid leaving the backlight on continuously. Always carry enough sets of spare batteries to last the trip.

Use all means of navigation at your disposal, not just GPS. On a trail, for example, pay attention to trail signs and keep track of prominent landmarks, using your map. Take notes in a small notebook or on your map as you progress. When hiking cross-country, chart your progress on the map with a pencil. If you save GPS waypoints, write the coordinates or the name of the waypoint on the map or in your notebook.

DETERMINING YOUR POSITION

If you are in a vehicle and you are not using an external antenna, you may have to stop and use the receiver outside. Try to get the best view of the sky possible from your location. In dense forest, find a clearing or an opening in the canopy. Stay away from cliffs—they can reflect the satellite signal and cause false readings.

When first turned on, the receiver displays a status page that tells you how many satellites are visible and how strong their signals are. The visible satellite display is usually a small map of the sky, with the horizon represented by the outer ring of a circle and the 45-degree elevation above the horizon by an inner circle. Each satellite is marked with its PRN number (a unique number assigned to each satellite), and reversing the display colors indicates satellites being received. A satellite is considered visible when it is above the masking angle (normally, 10 degrees above the horizon). A separate display gives the signal strength of each satellite by its PRN number. The GPS receiver must receive at least four satellites to calculate your position accurately. The position of the satellites is important. GPS position fixes are most accurate when three of the satellites are just above the masking angle, spread evenly along the horizon, and a fourth satellite is directly overhead. GPS positions are least accurate when the four satellites are close together in the sky—a condition called poor satellite geometry. Most receivers provide some indication of the accuracy of the fix. Some use a warning icon to indicate poor satellite geometry; others display a numerical value, such as feet, to indicate the accuracy level.

When the receiver is first used after a period of months, or if it has been moved several hundred miles since the last use, it may take from 5 to 15 minutes to get a fix. This is because the almanac data showing the approximate positions of the satellites is out of date. The receiver updates this information from the satellite transmissions. Most receivers allow you to enter an approximate position (the nearest city, for example) to help speed up the process. Most receivers call this initialization or sky search.

If the GPS receiver has been used recently but not within the last 30 minutes, it will perform a cold start. This means it has to wait for the satellites to broadcast their ephemeris data, which gives the precise location of the satellites. This happens quickly; most receivers will get a fix within a minute or two from a cold start. A warm start is the fastest of all. If the receiver has been used in the last 30 minutes, it will get a fix in 15 seconds to a minute.

If there are any sky obstructions, it helps to be stationary when getting a fix. This is because momentary interruptions in the signal may make the entire almanac or ephemeris message invalid, and the GPS receiver has to start over. Parallel channel receivers are faster than multiplexing receivers in getting the first fix. They also maintain their lock better when moving.

Once the GPS receiver has enough satellites for a fix, it will switch to the position page, which shows your current position and usually your altitude and the time. If you are moving, the position page on most receivers also shows your track (your heading or actual direction of travel) and your speed. The position page may also show a compass rose or heading tape (a horizontal scale with a tick mark at your heading) to help you visualize your heading. If the GPS receiver cannot receive at least four satellites, it will display a warning that it is doing 2-D navigation, and it may ask you to enter your altitude. Do not rely on 2-D navigation unless you are going to be at a constant, known elevation, such as on water. Some GPS receivers do not allow you to enter an altitude; they assume you are at sea level or the last computed altitude. Errors of several miles can result from using 2-D navigation on land.

The receiver will start 3-D navigation as soon as it receives four satellites. Some receivers do not have obvious warnings that they are in 2-D mode. It is essential that you know how to determine if your receiver is in 2-D or 3-D mode.

Occasionally you will have problems fixing a position. The receiver will warn you on the display and will possibly sound an audible alarm. The usual cause is a poor view of the sky. Since the satellite signals are received strictly in the line of sight, even widely spaced trees can block reception. Deep, narrow canyons are especially difficult spots from which to fix your position. The best locations are open meadows or clearings with low horizons. If you have to get a fix in forest cover, move around to get the strongest signal strengths on the status page. Once you do have a fix, do not move until you have saved your position, or checked the bearings to your next waypoint, especially if there are overhead obstacles. Occasionally, you will not be able to get a fix at all because of poor satellite geometry. Since the satellites are moving, often you will be able to get a fix after waiting a few minutes. Sometimes, turning the receiver off and on again will reset it and it will lock on.

FINDING YOUR POSITION ON A MAP

To find your position on a map with coordinates read from your GPS receiver, reverse the procedures described earlier for reading coordinates from a map (see page 39). If possible, cross-check the GPS position by finding your location through some other means, such as with nearby landmarks— a road, trail signs, etc. If you are in circumstances where GPS is your only means of navigation (in cases of fog, featureless terrain, or whiteout conditions), take GPS fixes more often and compare them to each other.

Caution: *Never depend on a single, unverified GPS position in a critical situation.*

Remember that the accuracy of civilian GPS is 330 feet (100 meters or 0.06 miles) horizontally. This means that GPS positions can be as far as 330 feet from the actual positions. Some newer GPS receivers have a position-averaging feature, which improves the accuracy of fixes by averaging a series of fixes over time. Accuracy of 50 feet or better is claimed. To use this feature, you must be stationary.

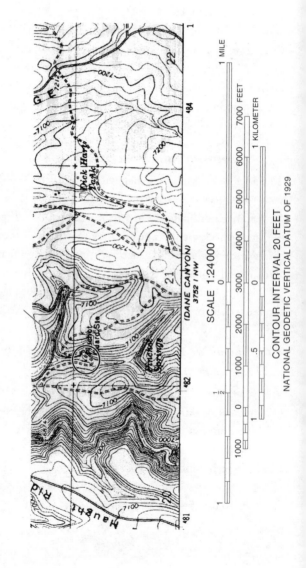

Figure 9: GPS position accuracy on a 7.5-minute map

SAVING YOUR POSITION AS A WAYPOINT

You can save your current position as a waypoint any time the receiver is locked on. Most receivers give you a choice of naming the waypoint yourself or having the receiver automatically assign it a name. The automatic feature is useful if you are in a hurry. (Some receivers have a "man overboard" function for quickly saving a position and then automatically starting navigation back to that point.) The receiver assigns sequential numbers to waypoints as you enter them. Some receivers also stamp waypoints with the date and time, which can help in remembering the purpose of a waypoint later. In most cases, it is best to name waypoints yourself. GPS receivers allow five or six characters for the name; most have a short description also. You may want to make notes on your map or in a small notebook to describe the waypoint more fully than you can in the receiver's memory.

The datum and coordinate system settings do not matter when creating a waypoint by saving your current position, because the receiver always uses WGS84 to save positions. The receiver converts from WGS84 to the currently selected datum and coordinate systems to display your current position and the location of waypoints. That is why it's so critical to have set the correct datum and coordinate system when plotting coordinates on a map or reading coordinates from a map for entry into the receiver.

NAVIGATING TO A WAYPOINT

To navigate to a waypoint, use the receiver's "GoTo" function to select the desired waypoint. After you have selected a waypoint, the receiver immediately starts navigating from your present position to the chosen waypoint, giving you a choice of several pages of navigation information. The primary page to use while navigating, naturally enough, is the navigation page. (Some receivers have several different navigation pages, each showing different combinations of information. Often you can customize one or more of these pages.) The navigation page shows bearing and distance to the next waypoint from your present position, and your track and speed. If you are exactly on course, your track and the bearing to the waypoint will be the same. Of course, if you are driving on a road, you have to stick to the road system. Still, the track information shows you if your current road is taking you in the general direction of your destination. When you reach a crossroads, the bearing tells you which way to turn.

Another item on the navigation page is estimated time en route (ETE) to the waypoint. Some receivers may also show an estimated time of arrival (ETA) at the waypoint. ETE and ETA are computed from your current speed toward the waypoint. This is called velocity made good, or VMG. As you travel, following a road or a trail or dodging obstacles, you are not always headed directly toward the next waypoint. Thus, your rate of progress toward a waypoint is less than your actual speed across the ground. As your actual track (track made good, or TMG) twists and turns, your

VMG changes and so does your ETA. Some GPS receivers allow you to average the velocity over a short period. Otherwise, you can check the ETA occasionally and average it in your head. This knowledge can be useful in figuring out, for example, if you will be able to drive to the trailhead before dark. If you were planning to camp at the trailhead and your ETA shows you will not make it during daylight, you might want to look for a closer place to camp.

Most GPS receivers have a plot page that shows your position in relation to waypoints. Your course (also called the desired track, or DTK) is shown as a straight line from waypoint to waypoint along your current leg. Your TMG is also shown as you progress. Often, bearing and distance to the next waypoint are shown along with heading (your current direction of travel) and speed. The plot page gives you an easy-to-understand graphic of your navigational picture. On many receivers, a database of geographic information allows the plot to show major roads and cities as well as other features. Aviation and marine GPS receivers have specialized databases showing airports, navigation stations, and other information useful for navigating in the air or on water. These databases allow the receiver to present a true moving map.

As you progress, the display updates the navigation information at least once a second. The GPS receiver will display a warning on the screen when you are approaching a waypoint. Most receivers can be set to give an audible warning as well.

At low speeds (under 10-15 miles per hour), GPS receivers may not compute speed consistently due to the accuracy limits of the GPS system. If the displayed speed and ETA are fluctuating as you move, you either have to average them in your head or ignore them. Some receivers have an averaging function to smooth out the speed, making them more useful at low speeds. Still, the best way to navigate at slow speeds (when walking, bicycling, paddling, skiing, etc.) is to use the receiver while stopped. Get a position fix, save it as a waypoint if necessary, note the bearing and distance to the next waypoint, then shut the receiver off. Use your compass, the sun, or the lay of the land to determine your direction, then use landmarks or the compass to maintain that direction as you travel.

6

Trail Hiking

Before leaving a trailhead, always save your vehicle's position as a waypoint and name it something unmistakable, such as TRUCK or TRAILH. That way, you will be able to find your vehicle even without a map.

It is difficult to use a GPS receiver as you travel. The receiver must be held in a position where its antenna has access to the sky. The normal twists and turns of the hiking trail can cause the receiver to lose its lock. For survey, mapping, and other specialized work, a pack-mounted antenna is used to overcome these difficulties. A more practical approach for backcountry users is to stop and take a fix periodically. This technique also saves batteries. Rest stops are an ideal time to use the receiver. You can get an updated fix and check the bearing and direction to your next waypoint. This is also a good time to cross-check your position on the map using both the GPS fix and the map and compass.

On the trail, it helps to have predefined waypoints and routes set up at home before the trip or at camp. Of course, you can enter new waypoints at any time using your map and the methods described earlier or by saving your current position as a waypoint. In the field, especially in bad weather, it may be easier to define a new waypoint using distance and direction from an existing waypoint.

Even if you do not plan to actively navigate using your GPS receiver, save waypoints at important trail junctions and landmarks such as stream crossings, passes, campsites, etc. That way you will have the GPS navigation information if you lose the trail or become disoriented.

Cross-Country Hiking

Hiking cross-country usually involves making continuous small detours to avoid obstacles. The classic navigation technique is to pick a distant landmark in the direction you need to go and travel toward it, and you should do this as a back-up to GPS. Of course, this does not work in dense forest or fog. The GPS receiver replaces the distant visual landmark with an electronic one that is unaffected by weather. Each time you turn the receiver on, it tells you the direction to your next waypoint from your current position, no matter how much you have had to deviate from the straight-line course. It also shows you how far off course you are, and in which direction.

When cross-country hiking, generally you will select the same landmarks you would use without a GPS receiver. For example, you might plan to hike a trail for a few miles, then strike off cross-country to a good fishing lake. In this case, set up waypoints at the trailhead, the point where you will leave the trail, and the lake. Then set up a route using these three waypoints. As you hike, stop periodically and check your progress with the GPS receiver. As you near the point where you will leave the trail, you may want to leave the receiver on so that you do not miss the turnoff. When the receiver detects that you have reached the turnoff waypoint, it automatically navigates to the next waypoint—in this case, the lake.

Backtracking is made easier by the route reversal feature on most GPS receivers. In the example above, reversing the route creates a route from the lake to the trailhead with an intermediate waypoint at the point where you will rejoin the trail. Some receivers let you create a route from the automatically stored track data. This function only works if you have left the receiver on continuously or have at least saved fixes at major turns in the route.

Triangulation can be used with the GPS receiver, map, and compass to identify an unknown landmark that you cannot reach; for example, a distant mountain peak that you would like to identify. First, determine your position with the receiver and mark it on your map. Using the compass, take a bearing on the landmark, then plot this bearing on the map. Draw a bearing line from your present position to the landmark. Now, travel far enough so that you are looking at the unknown landmark from a different angle—the closer you are to 90 degrees from the first position, the better. Use the GPS receiver to get your new position and mark it on the map. Take another compass sight on the landmark and plot the bearing line on the map. The two lines will intersect at the landmark.

Hiking the Cabin Loop

Let's say you want to drive to a trailhead, then hike a trail that's known to be difficult to find. In this example, we will set up waypoints and routes in advance for the drive to the trailhead and the hike, then use the GPS receiver to help find the trailhead and the trail.

PLANNING A DRIVE TO A TRAILHEAD: PINCHOT CABIN

Let us say you want to drive to Pinchot Cabin, a trailhead and a historic cabin near East Clear Creek in the forested Mogollon Plateau country of central Arizona. First, find the waypoints you will need on your map: one for the highway turnoff, one for the cabin, and one for each major road junction on the way in, and enter them into the receiver.

All routes must have a starting and ending waypoint, and you will probably need intermediate waypoints unless you plan to travel in a straight line. Most GPS receivers can store several routes, each consisting of multiple waypoints, but only one route at a time can be actively used for navigation. Also, routes can be inverted, or reversed, for the return trip, so that you do not have to reenter the route data just to backtrack. A **route-editing** feature allows you to edit an

Figure 10: Trailhead route with GPS waypoints

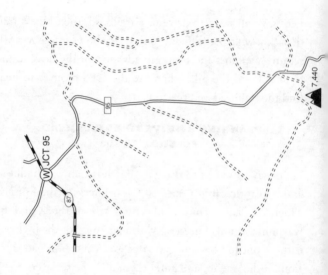

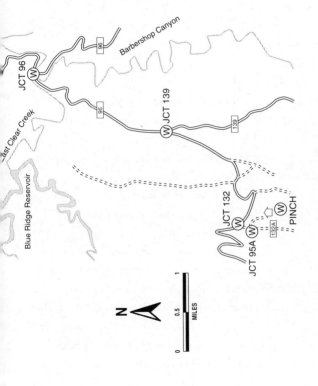

Barbershop Canyon

96

JCT 96 Ⓦ

East Clear Creek

95

Ⓦ JCT 139

139

Blue Ridge Reservoir

JCT 132 Ⓦ

132A

Ⓦ PINCH

JCT 95A Ⓦ

N

0   0.5   1
MILES

71

Figure 11: Waypoints along the road to Pinchot Cabin

```
ROUTE: 1
AZ87-PINCHOT
NO WAYPNT DTK DIS
1. JCT95
             163  4.6
2. JCT96
             201  2.0
3. JCT139
             235  1.4
4. JCT132
             179  0.1
5. JCT95A
             153  0.2
6. PINCH
7. ____     ___  ___
```

existing route, adding, changing, or deleting waypoints. The route-editing screen usually shows the azimuth and distance to each waypoint from the preceding one, and the total distance of the route.

This is valuable information for trip planning even if you do not actually use the GPS to navigate. Keep in mind that the total distance shown on the route screen is shorter than the actual road or trail distance on the ground. Another advantage of using the route feature is that the receiver remembers the active route when turned off and resumes navigating the route the next time it is turned on. If you use the GoTo function to navigate to a waypoint, most receivers cancel the GoTo when turned off.

Next, define a route using the waypoints you have just entered. You will need to select the waypoint for each leg (segment between waypoints) of the route. To specify a waypoint, most receivers present a blank waypoint field, then let you scroll through characters with the up/down arrow keys. The left/right arrow keys let you move to the next character position. Most receivers show the first waypoint that matches the characters you have entered so far. You can also scroll through an alphabetical list of waypoints. Some receivers have a "nearest waypoint" list that presents waypoints sorted by their distance from your current position. Call the route AZ87-PINCHOT. You should also make a few notes to go with the waypoints we have used to create the route.

If your route involves a loop with a **cherrystem** (a section of the route traveled both ways), the GPS receiver may get confused while you are navigating the cherrystem. It may be unable to tell whether you are outbound or inbound. To avoid this ambiguity, break the route into two separate routes in the receiver. End the first route partway around the loop section and start the second route with the last waypoint of the first route.

TABLE: *Pinchot Cabin trailhead route*

WAYPOINT	ACTION
JCT 95	From the west, turn right onto Forest Road 95, a maintained dirt road
JCT96	Turn right to stay on FR95, also maintained
JCT139	Go straight ahead, remaining on FR95
JCT132	Turn left on FR132, which may or may not be maintained
JCT95A	Left again on FR95A, the unmaintained spur road to the cabin
PINCH	Historic cabin

PLANNING A HIKE: THE CABIN LOOP TRAILS

For this example, we will use the Cabin Loop trails, which start from Pinchot Cabin, the destination in the last example. This system of USDA Forest Service trails follows the route of three historic trails. The USDAFS has recently retraced the routes of these trails, which date from the pioneer days. You know from talking to an experienced friend who has done the hike that the route can be hard to find. The terrain is a pine-forested plateau cut by numerous shallow canyons. The broad ridges between the canyons have been logged in the past and are laced with a network of forest roads. In places, the route follows old roads; in other places, it follows blazes on the trees. The trail is distinct in some sections but faint or nonexistent in others. Due to the length of the loop, you plan to do it as an overnight hike, allowing plenty of time for the approach drive, as well as time to explore the historic sites along the hiking route. Because most of the canyons are dry, it is important to find the springs along the route. You would also like to make sure you find the historic cabins and the old trail construction at the canyon crossings.

Before leaving home, you use the two USGS topographic maps of the area, Dane Canyon and Blue Ridge Reservoir, to map out the trails as well as you can. You use a UTM grid reader to create waypoints at the critical points and name the waypoints appropriately. As you create the waypoints, you make notes to remind you of their purpose once you are in the field. The first waypoint, PINCH, marks the trail-head near Pinchot Cabin, the first historic site. During the hike, you will be able to judge your progress around the loop by checking the distance and direction to PINCH.

The next waypoint, BARBER, marks the point where the U-Bar Trail crosses Barbershop Canyon. You know that the section of trail leading to Barbershop Canyon is actually just a line of tree blazes, which could be easy to lose in the forest. You also want to make sure you find the crossing, which has a fine example of the original trail construction dating from over a hundred years ago. Beyond the crossing, the trail intermittently follows several roads, then passes McClintock Spring. You put a waypoint, MCCLNT, at the spring. Next, the trail crosses Dane Canyon. This is another historic section of the old trail, and there is permanent water flowing here , so you mark the spot with the DANECN waypoint. Now the U-Bar trail turns south along the rim of Dane Canyon, passing Dane Spring and the ruins of another old cabin. You mark the spring with another waypoint, DANESP. About 2 miles farther south, the U-Bar Trail ends at its junction with the Barbershop Trail near Coyote Spring. You mark this junction with the COYOTE waypoint.

Here you will want to take a short side trip to Buck Springs Cabin, less than a mile to the east. You mark the site with a waypoint called BUCK. A spring near the old cabin can provide fresh water.

The main hike continues west along the Barbershop Trail, which crosses the heads of several canyons. The most important of these is Barbershop Canyon. Though you

Figure 12: Finding a historic trail with GPS

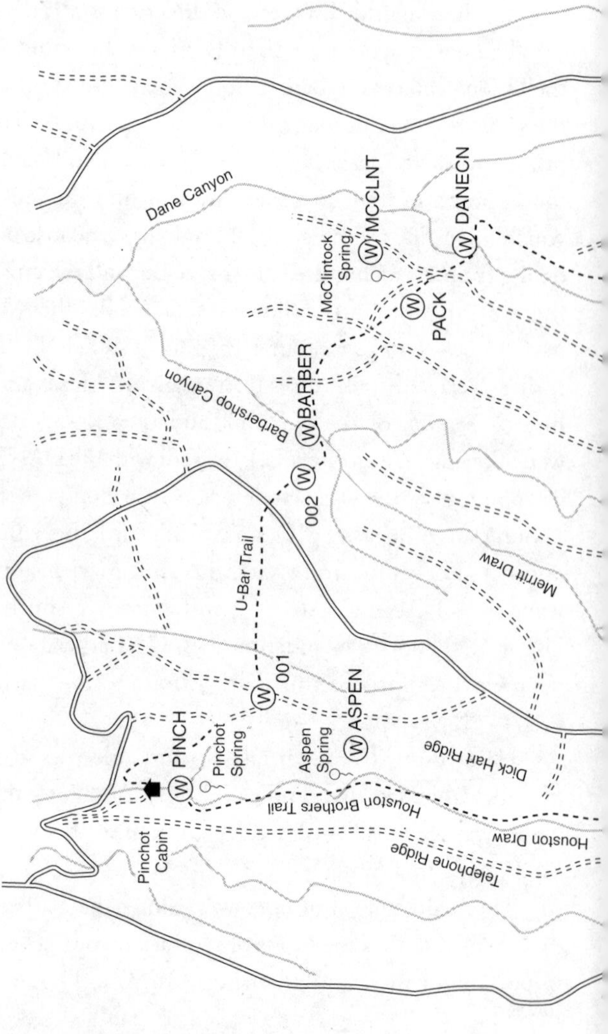

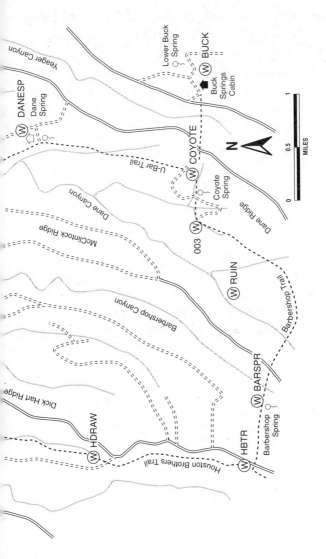

expect the canyon to be dry at this point , Barbershop Spring is located a few hundred yards west of the main drainage. This spring is important because you may not find water again until near the trailhead. You mark it with the BARSPR waypoint. Less than a mile beyond the spring, you will cross a dirt road, then meet the Houston Brothers Trail. Since this will be your return trail, you mark it with the HBTR waypoint.

The trail turns north along Telephone Ridge, parallel-ing the road, then crosses a branch road and drops into shallow Houston Draw. To stay on the historic route, you must find the right drainage, so you mark this point with a waypoint name HDRAW. You place your final waypoint at Aspen Spring and call it ASPEN. When you pass the spring, you will be about a mile from the trailhead at PINCH. Fi-nally, you use all the waypoints to create a route named CABIN LOOP that reads PINCH, BARBER, MCCLNT, DANECN, DANESP, COYOTE, BUCK, COYOTE, BARSPR, HBTR, HDRAW, ASPEN, and PINCH. Note that COYOTE is entered twice because you will be back-tracking after BUCK. Since the hike is a loop, PINCH is used as the starting and ending waypoint of the route.

TABLE: *Cabin Loop hike route*

WAYPOINT	ACTION
PINCH	Pinchot Cabin and the trailhead (also the final waypoint of approach route)
BARBER	Cross Barbershop Canyon—look for historic trail construction on both sides
MCCLNT	McClintock Spring—possible water; exact route of trail not known in this area
DANECN	Cross Dane Canyon—permanent water and historic trail construction
DANESP	Old cabin and possible water source. Should be an access road to this point
COYOTE	Junction with Barbershop Trail. Go left for side trip to Buck Springs Cabin. On return, look for Coyote Spring a few yards west
BUCK	Buck Springs Cabin and spring
BARSPR	Barbershop Spring—pick up water here and plan to camp a short distance beyond
HBTR	Junction with Houston Brothers Trail— turn right
HDRAW	Trail crosses a road and descends into Houston Draw—must find correct draw
ASPEN	Historic spring

DRIVING TO THE PINCHOT CABIN TRAILHEAD

For this example, we will use the waypoints and route we set up earlier to find Pinchot Cabin via the forest road system. After setting up the external antenna and connecting the GPS receiver to a power source, turn the receiver on. Assuming that you have some miles to go to reach the highway turnoff (waypoint JCT95), use the GoTo function and the navigation page to track your progress toward JCT95. You will use a highway map and a forest map to navigate to the turnoff, but the GPS display provides useful information as you drive. Knowing the bearing and distance to JCT95 allows you to judge your progress. Your track should generally be the same as the bearing, allowing for twists and turns in the road. A large discrepancy in your track might mean you have taken a wrong turn. The estimated time of arrival (ETA) tells you when you can expect to arrive at the turnoff, at your present rate of travel. The ETA changes constantly as your track and speed change, so you will need to average it over time. You can check your velocity made good (VMG) to see how fast you are actually traveling toward JCT95.

The most useful piece of information the receiver provides is the distance to the waypoint. When you get within a mile or so, you will know to start watching for the turnoff. Most receivers have an arrival alarm that sounds or flashes when you are approaching the destination waypoint. An audible alarm is especially useful if you do not have a passenger to navigate for you.

After turning right onto Forest Road 95, activate the AZ87-PINCHOT route you created earlier, then continue along FR 95. The receiver detects that you are between the JCT95 and JCT96 waypoints, and correctly assumes that you want to navigate from JCT95 to JCT96. Again, you can judge your progress using the navigation page. The plot or map screen shows your actual track as you follow the road, and the desired track from JCT95 to JCT96. You know the next turn will be onto a maintained road, so you ignore all the minor side roads.

The arrival alarm warns that you are approaching JCT 96. The road junction appears when the receiver says you are 0.05 miles from it, which is within the accuracy limits of GPS. There are no road signs at the junction. Stopping to check your notes, you see that you should turn right. The receiver's navigation page has jumped to the next waypoint, JCT139, and gives a bearing of 202 degrees. Your current heading is 162 degrees, confirming that you should turn right. Some navigation pages will let you display turn information, which the receiver automatically computes as the difference between the bearing to the waypoint and your actual track. Your turn display says you should turn 40 degrees right. The forest map agrees, so you turn right and continue.

At the next road junction, JCT 139, the receiver's turn display tells you to turn 34 degrees right. Your notes say to go straight ahead to remain on FR 95. You continue straight ahead and follow FR 95 as it curves right.

When you reach the next waypoint, JCT 132, you know

from your notes and the receiver to turn left. You do not know if FR 132 is a major or minor road, or if it is signed. In addition, the map shows quite a few side roads in the area, and you know that you are close to the cabin. To make it easier to navigate to the cabin, you switch to the plot page and zoom the display to 0.5 mile. Now you can clearly see your present position at JCT 132 and the final two way-points, including the cabin. FR 132 turns out to be an unmarked minor road; you turn left.

You know that the next turnoff, waypoint JCT 95A, is an obscure, unsigned road, so you watch the GPS carefully. Find the turnoff and go left. Now the receiver shows that the cabin is just 0.2 miles ahead. The road winds down a slope into a shallow draw, and there on the edge of a meadow is the old cabin.

HIKING THE CABIN LOOP

At the trailhead at Pinchot Cabin, switch on the receiver and allow it extra time to get a good fix. If you have a posi-tion-averaging feature, use it. You want to make sure the trailhead fix is as accurate as possible. Save the fix and call it TRAILH. Now, check the accuracy of the PINCH waypoint you entered at home. In most receivers, you can do this by selecting the waypoint from the waypoint list. The waypoint page shows the coordinates of the waypoint, but more im-portantly in this case, it shows the bearing and distance to the waypoint from your current position. The display now shows that you are 0.02 miles from PINCH, which is well within the 0.06-mile accuracy limits of GPS. As another check, look at the TRAILH waypoint we just saved. It shows a distance of 0.05 miles, still within the accuracy limits. You now have two waypoints marked at the trailhead you can use to find your way back, if necessary.

Now, activate the CABIN LOOP route you created earlier. Switching to the plot page, you change the scale so that you can see the entire route. This serves as a double check to make sure no waypoints are entered incorrectly. If a waypoint is off by a significant amount, it will be obvious on the plot screen. Now, you zoom the map to the 5-mile scale, which shows the next waypoint, BARBER. In doing this, you notice the screen is cluttered by the track you made on the drive to the trailhead, so you use the clear track function from the receiver's menu to erase the old track. Now the only lines on the plot screen are the desired track lines between waypoints on the Cabin Loop.

With the GPS receiver turned off but handy in its case on your belt, you start up the U-Bar Trail. It climbs up the east side of the draw onto the forested plateau. The tread is distinct and you note the blazes on the trees. Before long the trail merges with an old road, so you follow the road, keeping an eye out for blazes. Another road soon joins from the left, and a few yards farther on, the tree blazes suddenly veer left, away from the road. There is no sign of trail tread on the flat, needle-carpeted forest floor. You turn on the receiver and check the direction to BARBER. Checking direction by the sun, the blazes look as if they are headed in the right direction, but you get out your compass and check the bearing to BARBER to confirm. Just as a precaution, you save your current position as a waypoint, letting the receiver automatically name it 001. You note the waypoint on your topographic map. This waypoint will allow you to find this junction again—the last place where you were positive of being on the trail.

Turning the receiver off, you follow the blazes east through the pine forest. The route crosses a major drainage and, about a half an hour later, a major dirt road shown on the map. You follow the blazes for a short distance further, then lose them in an area of freshly downed trees. You check the receiver for the bearing and distance to BARBER. You are less than half a mile from the canyon crossing. Since you are anxious to find the trail again so you do not miss the trail construction in Barbershop Canyon, you use your compass to walk the bearing to BARBER. (Again, make sure you are using the same north reference with compass and GPS—preferably true north.) Soon you reach the rim of the small canyon. There is no sign of the trail. Checking the receiver again, you see that BARBER is upstream, or south, from your location. You decide to walk the rim to see if you will intercept the trail. Sure enough, you find the blazed route again and the obvious trail construction. You mark this point as waypoint 002, making a note on your map to remind you of its purpose.

The trail is obvious as it descends into the canyon. At the bottom, you take a rest break by the stream and check your position with the receiver. The BARBER waypoint is only 0.03 mile from your location, so you do not need to save a new waypoint. After a while you follow the trail as it climbs out the east side of the canyon. The blazes are easy to follow even after the trail construction disappears on the pine flats. It is less than a mile to McClintock Spring, so you keep an eye on the time. After half an hour, you will have traveled a mile and should be near the spring, so you stop and check the receiver. The receiver is now navigating to MCCLNT, the next waypoint on the route. It shows the spring bearing east at 89 degrees true and 0.3 miles away. The trail, however, is heading southeast at 140 degrees. Leaving the receiver on, you walk along the trail until the spring bears 45 degrees and is 0.25 miles away. It becomes clear that the spring is a short distance from the trail but not actually on it.

Deciding to find the spring and refill your water bottles, you save a waypoint to mark your location and name it PACK. Leaving your pack beside a blazed tree, but taking the receiver, map, and compass, you walk northeast through the forest and find the spring in less than 15 minutes. After filling your bottles, you activate GoTo navigation to PACK and note the bearing, 227 degrees, and the distance, 0.28 miles. Using the sun to estimate the direction, you walk southwest and back to your pack.

You continue along the trail, following it across Dane Canyon and then south along the rim. The trail is distinct in this section but you are concerned about missing the old cabin at Dane Spring if it is not on the trail, as was the case with McClintock Spring. You check the receiver after about 45 minutes of walking and it shows DANESP 0.45 miles distant at a bearing of 168 degrees. Using your compass, you see that the trail is heading almost directly toward the spring, at 166 degrees. The spring is probably very near the trail, unless the trail turns. Sure enough, after another 20 minutes of walking, you find the spring and the ruins of the old cabin at the end of a spur road that meets the trail.

Continuing along the U-Bar Trail as it heads south, you occasionally use the receiver to check your progress toward the next waypoint, COYOTE. You would like to reach the spring near the junction with the Barbershop Trail in time for lunch. You reach the trail junction and find the spring a couple of hundred yards to the west. After lunch, you leave your pack and follow the trail east to Buck Springs Cabin, which you find without difficulty. After checking out the cabin and nearby spring, you check your position with the receiver and find that the BUCK waypoint is correct. You hike back to your pack and continue east on the Barbershop Trail.

The trail, now just a line of blazed trees, wanders through an area of shallow draws laced with numerous old roads. Finally, you lose the trail entirely. Stopping at the last blazed tree you have been able to find, you turn on the receiver and save your position as waypoint 003. After looking at the topographic map, you decide to hike cross-country directly to Barbershop Spring, your planned campsite. The terrain is nearly flat and you will have only a few shallow canyons to cross. The receiver shows that the BARSPR waypoint is at 243 degrees, 1.9 miles away. You use your compass to check the direction, then set out.

Cross-country travel is easy through the open forest. You have been walking for just over half an hour when, descending into one of the shallow canyons, you spot the ruins of a log cabin alongside the drainage. The old structure is not marked on the topographic map. Checking the area, you cannot find a road or a trail leading to the cabin site. You would like to spend some time exploring, but it is late afternoon and time presses. Therefore, you use the receiver to save your position as a waypoint named RUIN and mark the location on your topographic map, using the UTM coordinates shown on the display. You plan to return later and use the saved waypoint to find the old cabin.

Resuming your cross-country walk toward Barbershop Spring, you walk for about 20 minutes before checking your progress on the receiver. The spring is now 0.3 mile away and the map shows that you should be crossing a major dirt road very shortly. Sure enough, you do, but there is still no sign of the trail. On the far side of the road you descend into a shallow canyon; this is probably the head of Barbershop Canyon. The GPS display confirms this, and as you continue toward the spring, you leave the receiver on. When it shows you already at the spring, you are standing on dry forest floor, but a shallow ravine lies ahead. As you descend into the ravine, you find a faint trail and distinct blazes on the trees leading to the west. You find the spring in the ravine and fill your water bottles. It is a damp, buggy place, and you prefer not to camp near springs anyway, so you hike a few hundred yards west on the trail and find a place to camp out of sight of both the trail and the spring.

Next morning, back on the trail, you check the receiver. The distance and bearing to the junction with the Houston Brothers Trail according to the map should be 0.5 miles west, and the receiver confirms that. The trail crosses a road, and you find the junction on the other side. Now you turn right and hike north. The next waypoint, HDRAW, marks the point where the trail descends into Houston Draw. The trail remains distinct, and you locate the head of the draw without difficulty. Still, you are glad you have the waypoint saved in the GPS receiver as a backup.

You know that Pinchot Cabin, the trailhead, is located in Houston Draw, so all you have to do is follow the draw north to reach it. Still, there are few landmarks in the upper part of the draw, so you check your progress on the receiver from time to time. You also want to make sure you find Aspen Spring. After an hour's steady hiking, you find a spring in an aspen grove. There is no sign, so you use the GPS to confirm that you are really at Aspen Spring. From here, it is an easy walk of less than a mile to Pinchot Cabin and the trailhead.

Exploring a Desert Mountain Range

GPS is especially handy when hiking or exploring cross-country. For the next example, a cross-country hike in the desert, you want to explore a desert mountain range that looks interesting on the map. According to your topographic map, the nearest vehicle access is a dirt road that parallels the range about 10 miles away. The only water source you know about is a natural tank that holds rainwater. Late winter seems a perfect time to go. It has been a wet winter, so the tank should be full, and now the weather is dry and cool—perfect for hiking. You plan to take three days on the trip because of the long walk across the desert to reach the foot of the range.

Since you do not know where you will want to park along the approach road, you cannot place a waypoint in advance. However, you do have a map location for the natural water tank, obtained from a Bureau of Land Management ranger. Since finding the water is critical to the success of your trip, you carefully determine the UTM coordinates and enter a waypoint called TANK into your GPS receiver. The tank is near the southern end of the section of the range you would like to explore, so you plan

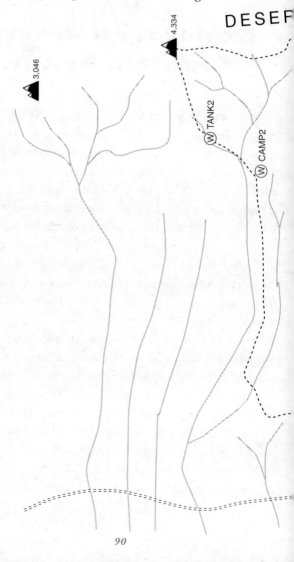

Figure 13: Exploring a desert mountain range

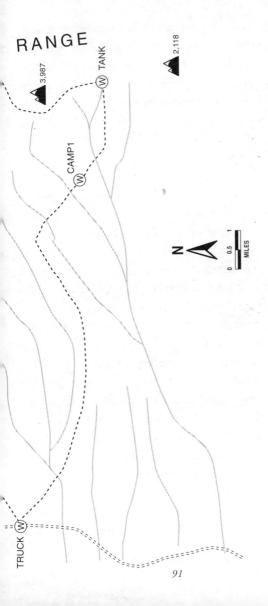

RANGE

▲ 3,987

Ⓦ TANK

▲ 2,118

Ⓦ CAMP1

N

0   0.5   1
MILES

Ⓦ TRUCK

to hike to the tank, then explore to the north before return-ing to your vehicle. Because of the length of the approach drive, you will probably not reach the tank the first night, so you plan to carry enough water for a dry camp. Connect your receiver to a power source in your vehicle before you set out. (You will have to get an accessory power cord to do this, which plugs into the cigarette lighter.)

As you drive along the desert road, you turn the receiver on, and set up TANK as a GoTo route. Then you switch to the plot screen and zoom until you can see both your present position and TANK. This allows you to see where you are in relation to the tank. You park your truck where the road is closest to TANK. Since your GPS receiver has been running continuously on the vehicle's power, you know that it should have a good position fix. After checking carefully to make sure the receiver is in 3-D–navigation mode and there are no warning messages, you save your position as a waypoint named TRUCK. You also plot your position on your map and write the coordinates in the map margin.

Next, you check the receiver's navigation page, which is showing the bearing and distance to the tank. You use your compass to sight along the GPS bearing to the tank and note a peak along the crest of the distant range. You will use the peak for general guidance as you cross the desert plain. You stash the receiver and compass in your pack and start hiking. The otherwise flat plain is cut by numerous dry wash-es, so you are constantly making small detours, but the distant peak keeps you heading in the right direction. As expected, the setting sun forces you to stop and camp just as you reach the foothills. The receiver shows the tank still 2 miles away.

In the morning, you check the receiver's bearing to TANK and use your compass to find the direction. The terrain looks rugged between you and the tank, so you skirt it to the south. When you judge by the terrain and the time that you have gone about halfway to the tank, you switch the receiver on, check the bearing and distance, then hike directly toward the tank. You find it easily, and it is a welcome sight in the otherwise dry canyon. You check that the TANK waypoint is accurately located, then continue north along the range. Since your plan is to hike up to the crest of the range and work your way north to the highest peak, you navigate by the terrain and do not use your receiver.

After climbing the peak late in the day, you descend the southwest slopes in the general direction of your truck. You have enough water for another dry camp, so you plan to descend to the foothills and look for a campsite. While hiking down a dry wash, you find another natural water tank. It is smaller than the original tank, but worth knowing about, so you turn on your receiver and save your position as a new waypoint, TANK2. You also check your position with nearby landmarks, then mark the tank's location on your map. You pick up some extra water, then continue another mile or two to camp.

In the morning, you use the receiver to determine the direction and distance to your truck. Since there are no landmarks in that direction, you will maintain your course using the sun. You are not concerned about maintaining exact direction because you know the terrain will force you off course anyway. Sure enough, you quickly see that the low ridge you camped on offers the easiest way down. It takes you almost directly west, then slightly northwest before the going becomes easier. Taking a break, you again use the receiver to find the direction to your truck. This time you keep the receiver and compass handy as you hike because the desert is nearly flat here. You can only see about half a mile ahead because of the low brush lining the numerous dry washes. You maintain your course with the compass, stopping to check your progress occasionally with the receiver. Soon you spot your truck.

While this hike could certainly have been done without GPS, satellite navigation made it easier and faster to find the critical water tank. Then, GPS freed you to explore at will along the range, knowing that you could get out of the mountains and hike directly to your vehicle at any time. Without GPS, you would have had to keep track of your position carefully, and then deliberately hike toward a point well to one side of your truck so that you would know which way to turn when you hit the road. Finally, with GPS, you were able to mark the exact location of the new water tank, which will make it easier to explore the northern section of the range on a later trip.

Mapping a Mountain Bike Trail

In this example, you are a member of a mountain bike club that has just finished building a new bike trail in cooperation with the state parks. The trail wanders through dense forest with few landmarks. The park rangers would like your club to map the trail as accurately as possible for their records. The club would like a good map of the trail for its members and other riders.

To make the map, you ride the trail with a topographic map of the area, a compass, and a GPS receiver. You also have a cyclometer mounted on your bike so you can accurately measure distances on the trail. The odometer on your receiver is not as accurate because it only works when the receiver is on and while moving at speeds faster than 10 to 15 mph. You save a waypoint at the trailhead, of course, then ride the trail. At each intersection or major turn in the trail, you save a waypoint and note your mileage on the cyclometer. Before saving each waypoint, use the position-averaging feature of your receiver, waiting a few seconds for the receiver to compute a more accurate position. If the trail continues in the same direction for a while, you measure the bearing with your compass and record it.

Back at home, you plot all the GPS waypoints on your map using a UTM grid reader, then draw in the trail. The compass bearings help you align the trail through each waypoint. The cyclometer mileage can be used to develop a trail log that tells other cyclometer-equipped riders when to turn, etc. It can also serve as a cross-check on your GPS waypoints by seeing if the mileage between waypoints on the map agrees with the cyclometer distance. Remember to allow for twists and turns in the trail; the straight-line GPS distance will always be less than the trail distance unless the route is perfectly straight.

If you have a computer and mapping software, you can map a trail or any other route in even greater detail using the track log feature of your receiver. You will need to position the receiver so that it can get fixes while you ride. Though handlebar mounts are available, be aware that you could damage the receiver in a crash. You can probably put the receiver in a fanny pack or rear carrier bag so that the antenna has good access to the sky. Clear the track log before you start. As you ride the trail, manually save waypoints at intersections and other important points to back up the track log. If you use position averaging, the manual waypoints will be more accurate than the track log points.

At home, download the track log and waypoints to your computer. Use the mapping software to display the track and waypoints. With some software, you can draw a map on the screen. Otherwise, you can print your track and waypoints and use tracing paper to draw the map. Remember that the track fixes may be as far as 330 feet off the actual trail.

Even without a computer, the track log is useful as displayed on your receiver's plot screen. You can zoom and pan to show any section in detail and use the graphic display to help you draw your map.

Relocating Your Favorite Fishing Spot

Before doing any water travel with GPS, learn how to use your receiver's man overboard function (MOB), if it has one. When activated, this feature instantly saves a waypoint, then starts navigation to that waypoint. Although intended for larger boats that take some time and distance to maneuver back to the marked point, MOB can be useful for lake paddlers and anglers. To be useful, MOB should be activated with a button on the receiver, not buried deep in a menu system.

For flatwater navigation, it helps to mount your receiver so you can check it easily. It is not necessary to leave it on all the time—you can still keep the receiver off except for position and course checks. You should have a fully water-proof GPS receiver. If you are not certain your receiver is waterproof, you can protect it in a waterproof bag with a transparent cover that is specially made for handheld receivers. Although it's harder to operate the receiver through the bag, it provides attachment points to secure it to the boat or your gear, and the bag keeps the GPS afloat if it does fall in the water.

For example, let's say you want to paddle your canoe across a large lake to reach a favorite fishing spot and campsite on the far side. The distance is about 5 miles and there are no landmarks on the far shore to steer by. Last time you were at the spot, you saved a waypoint called FISH. Before setting out, save your launching point as a waypoint called LAUNCH, then create and activate a route from LAUNCH to FISH. As you paddle, the navigation page shows the bearing and distance to your goal. You can use the track information to stay on course, turning until your track and the bearing agree, but an easier method is to use the course deviation indicator (CDI), shown on one of your navigation pages. The CDI is usually a horizontal row of dots with a vertical bar or arrow. (Some receivers use a graphic of a road with a symbol representing your position.) The bar moves left or right to show how far off course you are. The scale of the CDI can be changed on the setup page. The CDI is not used much for land travel but can be very helpful for direct travel by water or air.

Set the CDI to its most sensitive scale. When you are on course, the course marker stays centered. If you get off course, the course marker moves to the side. Since the course marker represents your desired course, always turn toward it to get back on course. Make a small change in your heading and see if the CDI starts to center. If it doesn't, make another small heading change. When the CDI starts to move toward center, hold that heading until it has centered. If you make large changes, you will probably find yourself zigzagging through your course.

The cross track error (XTK) display shows distance off course. You can use XTK to help you decide how far to turn to get back on course. For example, if your destination is 5 miles away and your XTK is 0.1 miles, make a small turn, say 10 degrees, to get back on course. On the other hand, if your XTK is 1 mile and you have 5 miles to go, you should turn a larger turn, say 30 degrees, to get back on course. The idea is to get back on course without going too far out of your way.

If you have wind or current from one side, you will be carried off course even if your heading is the same as the bearing to the waypoint. In this case, steer a few degrees into the wind or current to compensate. Check the CDI occasionally; if you are off course, adjust your heading toward your desired course to correct yourself. If the wind or current is steady, you will be able to find a heading that keeps you exactly on course, so that you paddle the shortest distance to your destination.

Since it can be difficult to judge distance on water, the estimated time of arrival (ETA) display can help you measure your progress. Remember that ETA is calculated from your speed made good and the distance remaining to your waypoint. If you slow down or wander off course a lot, your ETA will change.

Keep in mind that the heading and ETA displays may be inaccurate at low speeds on some receivers and do not make constant course changes in response to small changes in the display. If a distant landmark is available, steer by that to stay on course; otherwise, use a compass. Remember that GPS is only accurate to 330 feet; don't depend on GPS alone for navigation in close quarters, such as around rocks and shoals.

Figure 14: Cross track error on the water

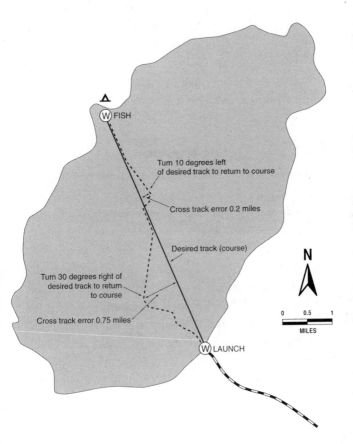

Advanced GPS

Some other aspects of GPS likely to interest backcountry users are PC mapping, the Automatic Position Reporting System (APRS), civilian vs. military accuracy, Differential GPS (DGPS), and the Wide Area Augmentation System (WAAS). Other applications, such as surveying and land management uses, are beyond the scope of this book. Refer to the appendix for books on these subjects.

PC MAPPING

PC mapping uses a GPS receiver and a personal computer to store, manipulate, and present GPS data. Such a system can function as a very accurate moving map and can be used to navigate to street addresses or businesses. Data can be collected in the field and used to map the location of roads or trails easily and accurately. GPS mapping has been the province of professionals due to the expensive hardware and software required, but now several inexpensive GPS mapping products bring this capability to general users. These products are based on digital USGS topographic data, which allow the software to compute and display exact coordinates and elevations for any position on the computer screen. See the Appendix for mapping software sources.

APRS

The Automatic Position Reporting System (APRS) is an amateur radio system developed for tracking objects with digital radio. APRS stations can be fixed, mobile, or portable, so the system can track all types of vehicles and even people. Since the system uses radio communications, general messages as well as specialized information such as weather observations can be transmitted. The Internet is also being used to link APRS stations, so it is not even necessary to have an amateur radio license to use APRS. An APRS station uses a computer to display a map with the positions of other APRS stations. Weather data and message traffic can be displayed.

Amateur radio operators are using APRS to provide communications and position tracking in disaster situations as well as for public service events such as races and parades. The Civil Air Patrol uses APRS to assist them in searching for overdue aircraft. For more information and an example of APRS in action, visit http://users.nbn.net/~gwells/index.html on the Internet.

CIVILIAN VERSUS MILITARY ACCURACY

Each satellite transmits three primary navigation signals: the C/A (course/acquisition) code, the P (precise) code, and the navigation signal. GPS's full accuracy is only available to P-code users—normally the military and selected civilians. These users enjoy horizontal positioning to 72 feet and altitude accuracy to 92 feet. For national security reasons, the civilian C/A code is degraded by the ground control stations, which deliberately introduce time errors into the satellite signal. This process is called Selective Availability (SA). The amount of error changes randomly, resulting in the specified accuracy of 328 feet horizontally and 512 feet vertically. Accuracy may be better than this at any given moment, and some newer GPS receivers, when stationary, can average positions over time, significantly improving accuracy. Still, an experienced map-reader in suitable terrain can often determine position more accurately than GPS degraded by SA.

The purpose of Selective Availability is to deny a potential enemy the use of precise GPS navigation. Since there are ways of increasing GPS accuracy without using the P-code, the value of Selective Availability seems dubious. In fact, the U.S. government has announced that Selective Availability will be phased out. To deny accurate GPS to an enemy, the military has been testing battlefield spoofing and jamming systems. Spoofing a GPS receiver fools it into giving false positions, while jamming prevents it from displaying any position at all.

DIFFERENTIAL GPS

Differential GPS (DGPS) overcomes the inaccuracy of the SA-degraded C/A code by using a GPS receiver and a DGPS beacon transmitter placed on a known, surveyed point. The DGPS transmitter continuously computes the difference between its known position and its GPS position, then transmits the correction. Field GPS receivers equipped with a DGPS receiver pick up this signal and correct their GPS location accordingly, achieving accuracy of 16 feet or better. DGPS adds complexity and cost to basic GPS: You must attach a DGPS beacon receiver to your normal GPS receiver, and even then it only works within range of a DGPS beacon transmitter.

DGPS is routinely used in surveying and will become increasingly important in navigation. The U.S. Coast Guard maintains a network of DGPS stations to improve the accuracy of marine navigation near the coast. The USDA Forest Service, the U.S. Bureau of Land Management, and other agencies, as well as private users, use DGPS locally to improve the accuracy of their survey and mapping operations.

WIDE AREA AUGMENTATION SYSTEM

The Wide Area Augmentation System (WAAS) is a DGPS system being built by the Federal Aviation Administration to improve the accuracy of GPS for aircraft en route between destinations. A similar system, the Local Area Augmentation System (LAAS), will be used for precision-instrument approaches so that aircraft can use GPS for guidance to the runway in bad weather. LAAS accuracy of better than an inch has been demonstrated in tests. Another function of both FAA DGPS systems is to warn flight crews of degraded accuracy or GPS failure. Such warnings are critical when GPS is being used to guide a fast-moving aircraft to a runway. WAAS will consist of a series of geostationary satellites and will transmit on the current GPS frequencies, so it will be available to anyone with a receiver capable of using the WAAS information. This will make very accurate DGPS available to all users.

The Future of GPS

GPS grew out of the military need for an accurate, 24-hour, global, all-weather navigation system that could provide rapidly updated positions for ships, aircraft, tanks, troops, and weapons. When planning started in 1973, the military had several major goals. The system had to be resistant to jamming, and it had to be encrypted (the radio signals had to be encoded) so that unauthorized persons could not interfere with it. The system also needed to be passive, so that the user did not have to reveal his position by transmitting. Civilian uses were not part of the original design, but many of the design features that make the system so useful to the military also make it attractive to civilians. The passive design means that GPS receivers are relatively simple devices, and their cost has dropped rapidly as electronic and computer technology improves.

The first GPS satellite, NAVSTAR 1, was launched in 1978, and its ten sisters followed it over the next few years. These early GPS satellites were prototypes, designed to test and refine the system. Though their design life was four and one-half years, some lasted more than twice that long. The next generation of GPS satellites began to be launched in 1989. These satellites are hardened against attack by antisatellite weapons and are designed with a seven-and-a-half-year lifetime. Yet a third generation of GPS satellites have more accurate atomic clocks and use intersatellite communications to reduce dependency on updates from ground stations.

In the future, GPS technology will become commonplace, much like calculators. Some people are concerned that GPS and other technologies such as cell and satellite telephones degrade or even destroy the wilderness experience. It is not a new argument. The same concern was expressed when the lightweight, high-tech aluminum pack frame was invented forty years ago. As a lifetime amateur radio operator, I have carried a small ham radio receiver in my pack for many years. I have had hiking companions object to the intrusion of two-way radio communications. The answer, as always, is to use technology that is appropriate to your backcountry trip. When I hike with non-ham companions, I leave the little radio out of sight in my pack, for use only in an emergency. Likewise, a GPS receiver can be kept in reserve in case the party becomes disoriented, in the same way as a compass is always carried but rarely used in open country.

Beware of becoming dependant on gadgets to get you out of trouble in wild country. In some areas—Utah's canyon country, for example, where the terrain is cut by thousands of canyons—GPS and compass navigation are utterly useless. While a GPS will tell you the direction and distance to your destination in a straight line, to get there you may have to hike many more miles and work closely with the terrain and a map to avoid canyons and other obstacles. Lastly, remember that electronic devices fail. Plan to rely on your own survival knowledge in the backcountry and use your high-tech equipment as a backup.

Resources

GPS COMPANIES

Adventure GPS Products, 220 E. Ave. K-4, Suite 4, Lancaster, CA 93535, (888) 477-4386, (805) 726-9474; info@gps4fun.com; http://www.gps4fun.com

ASC Scientific Company, 2075 Corte del Nogal, Suite G, Carlsbad, CA 92009, (800) 272-4327, (760) 431-2655; ascsci@ascsci.com; http://www.electriciti.com/geotools/index.html

GPS Store, P.O. Box 7659, South Brunswick, NC 28470, (910) 575-9544, (888) 477-2611; info@thegpsstore.com; http://www.thegpsstore.com

Map World, 123-D North El Camino Real, Encinitas, CA 92024, (760) 942-9642, (800) 246-6277; maps@mapworld.com; http://www.mapworld.com

Navtech Seminars and GPS Supply, Suite 400, 6121 Lincolnia Road, Alexandria, VA 22312-2707, (800) 628-0885, (703) 256-8900; gpsteach@navtechgps.com; http://www.navtechgps.com

Waypoint+, http://www.tapr.org/~kh2z/Waypoint/

GPS MANUFACTURERS

Garmin International, Inc., 1200 E. 151st Street, Olathe, KS 66062, (913) 397-8200; http://www.garmin.com

Lowrance/Eagle Electronics Inc., 12000 East Skelly Drive, Tulsa, OK 74128-2486, (800) 324-1356; http://www.lowrance.com; http://www.eaglegps.com (GPS receivers)

Magellan Systems Inc., 960 Overland Court, San Dimas, CA 91773, (909) 394-5000; http://www.magellangps.com

Micrologic Inc., 9174 Deering Avenue, Chatsworth, CA 91311, (818) 998-1216.

Raytheon Marine (Apelco), 676 Island Pond Road, Manchester, NH 03109-5420, (603) 647-7530, (800) 539-5539; http://www.apelco.com

Si-Tex Marine Electronics, Inc., 11001 Roosevelt Boulevard, Suite 800, St. Petersburg, FL 33716, (813) 576-5734; http://www.si-tex.com

Trimble Navigation Limited, 749 North Mary Avenue, Sunnyvale, CA 94086, (408) 481-8000; sales_info@trimble.com, http://www.trimble.com

COMPASS COMPANIES

Brunton Company, 620 East Monroe Avenue, Riverton, WY 82501, (307) 856-6559, (800) 443-4871; info@brunton.com; http://www.brunton.com

Silva Sweden AB, Kuskv_gen 4, 191 62 Sollentuna, Sweden, phone 46-8-623-43-00; info@silva.se; http://www.silva.se

Suunto USA Inc., 2151 Las Palmas Drive, Carlsbad, CA 92009, (800) 543-9124, suunto@ix.netcom.com; http://www.suuntousa.com.

MAP AND MAP SOFTWARE COMPANIES

Chicago Map Corporation, 15419 127th Street, Lemont, IL 60439, (800) 257-9244; mail@chicagomap.com; http://www.chicagomap.com

DeLorme (Street Atlas USA, Topo USA), Two DeLorme Drive, P.O. Box 298, Yarmouth, ME 04096, (800) 452-5931; info@delorme.com; http://www.delorme.com

Pinpoint Systems Inc. (Fugawi moving map software), 73 Warren Road, Suite 200, Toronto, Ontario M4V 2R9 Canada, (416) 920-0447; sales@fugawi.com; http://www.fugawi.com

US Geological Survey, Information Services, Box 25286, Denver, CO 80225, (800) HELP-MAP; http://mapping.usgs.gov

Wildflower Productions (TOPO! maps), 375 Alabama Street, Suite 230, San Francisco, CA 94110, (415) 558-8700; info@topo.com; http://www.info.com

GPS BOOKS AND MAGAZINES

GPS World, P.O. Box 6139, Duluth, MN 55806-6139, (800) 346-0085 x477; fulfil@superfil.com; http://www.gpsworld.com

BOOKS

Ferguson, Michael. *GPS Land Navigation.* Glassford Publishing: Boise, Idaho,1997. A detailed explanation of GPS, maps, and coordinate systems.

Greenhood, David. *Mapping.* University of Chicago Press: Chicago, 1964. This book has very readable coverage of coordinate systems, map projections, and map making.

Hofmann-Wellenhof, B. H. Lichtenegger, and J. Collins. *Global Positioning System: Theory and Practice.* Springer Verlag: New York, 1997. A comprehensive and technical look at GPS.

Kals, William S. *Land Navigation Handbook: The Sierra Club Guide to Map and Compass.* Sierra Club Books: San Francisco, 1983. Probably the best coverage of classic backcountry navigation with map, compass, and altimeter.

Kjellstrom, Bjorn. *Be Expert with Map and Compass.* Charles Scribner's Sons: New York, 1994. The classic work on orienteering, a competitive sport that uses map and compass to find preset marks on an orienteering course. Much of the information applies to backcountry navigation as well.

Larijani, L. Casey. *GPS for Everyone.* American Interface Corporation: New York, 1998. An up-to-date general survey of GPS and its uses.

Logston, Tom. *The Navstar Global Positioning System.* Van Nostrand Reinhold: New York, 1992. Good overview of GPS.

Sickle, Jan Van. *GPS for Land Surveyors.* Ann Arbor Press: Chelsea, Michigan, 1996. This is a moderately technical explanation of GPS and precision land survey.

Index

Page numbers in italics refer to illustrations.

N

O

P

About the Author

Bruce Grubbs is an avid hiker, mountain biker, paddler, and cross-country skier who has been exploring the American West for over 30 years. As a pilot, an amateur radio operator, and a mountain rescue team member, he has used high-technology gear in the backcountry for many years. He is a professional pilot with Airline Transport Pilot and Instrument Flight Instructor certificates. An outdoor writer and photographer, he has written eight other FalconGuides. He lives in Flagstaff, Arizona.

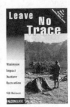

WILDLIFE VIEWING GUIDES

Alaska Wildlife Viewing Guide
Arizona Wildlife Viewing Guide
California Wildlife Viewing Guide
Colorado Wildlife Viewing Guide
Florida Wildlife Viewing Guide
Indiana Wildlife Vewing Guide
Iowa Wildlife Viewing Guide
Kentucky Wildlife Viewing Guide
Massachusetts Wildlife Viewing Guide
Montana Wildlife Viewing Guide
Nebraska Wildlife Viewing Guide
Nevada Wildlife Viewing Guide
New Hampshire Wildlife Viewing Guide

New Jersey Wildlife Viewing Guide
New Mexico Wildlife Viewing Guide
New York Wildlife Viewing Guide
North Carolina Wildlife Viewing Guide
North Dakota Wildlife Viewing Guide
Ohio Wildlife Viewing Guide
Oregon Wildlife Viewing Guide
Puerto Rico & the Virgin Islands
   Wildlife Viewing Guide
Tennessee Wildlife Viewing Guide
Texas Wildlife Viewing Guide
Utah Wildlife Viewing Guide
Vermont Wildlife Viewing Guide
Virginia Wildlife Viewing Guide
Washington Wildlife Viewing Guide
West Virginia Wildife Viewing Guide
Wisconsin Wildlife Viewing Guide

FALCONGUIDES®Leading the Way™

FALCONGUIDES® are available for where-to-go hiking, mountain biking, rock climbing, walking, scenic driving, fishing, rockhounding, paddling, birding, wildlife viewing, and camping. We also have FalconGuides on essential outdoor skills and subjects and field identification. The following titles are currently available, but this list grows every year. For a free catalog with a complete list of titles, call FALCON toll-free at 1-800-582-2665.

MOUNTAIN BIKING

Mountain Biking Arizona
Mountain Biking Colorado
Mountain Biking Georgia
Mountain Biking New Mexico
Mountain Biking New York
Mountain Biking Northern
  New England
Mountain Biking Oregon
Mountain Biking South Carolina
Mountain Biking Southern California
Mountain Biking Southern
  New England
Mountain Biking Utah
Mountain Biking Wisconsin
Mountain Biking Wyoming

LOCAL CYCLING SERIES

Fat Trax Bozeman
Mountain Biking Bend
Mountain Biking Boise
Mountain Biking Chequamegon
Mountain Biking Chico
Mountain Biking Colorado Springs
Mountain Biking Denver/Boulder
Mountain Biking Durango
Mountain Biking Flagstaff and
  Sedona
Mountain Biking Helena
Mountain Biking Moab
Mountain Biking White Mountains
Mountain Biking Utah's St. George/
  Cedar City Area

■ *To order any of these books, check with your local
bookseller or call FALCON* ® *at*
1-800-582-2665.
www.FalconOutdoors.com

FALCON®

FALCONGUIDES® Leading the Way™

FALCON®